Know It All!
Grades 3-5 Reading
by Jen Humphries

k12.princetonreview.com

Random House, Inc.
New York

www.randomhouse.com/princetonreview

This workbook was written by The Princeton Review, one of the nation's leaders in test preparation. The Princeton Review helps millions of students every year prepare for standardized assessments of all kinds. The Princeton Review offers the best way to help students excel on standardized tests.

The Princeton Review is not affiliated with Princeton University or Educational Testing Service.

Princeton Review Publishing, L.L.C.
160 Varick Street, 12th Floor
New York, NY 10013

E-mail: textbook@review.com

Published in the United States by Random House, Inc., New York.

ISBN 0-375-76378-3

Editor: Julia Munemo
Director of Production: Iam Williams
Design Director: Tina McMaster
Development Editor: Rachael Nevins
Art Director: Neil McMahon
Production Manager: Michael Rockwitz
Production Editor: Evangelos Vasilakis

Manufactured in the United States of America

9 8 7 6 5 4 3 2 1
First Edition

Contents

Parent and Teacher Introduction

About This Book

Know It All! focuses on the reading skills that students need to succeed in school and on standardized-achievement tests. This book provides accurate information about a wide array of fascinating subjects.

Know It All! contains chapters that cover important reading skills, regular reviews called "Brain Boosters," an answer key for the chapters and Brain Boosters, practice test, and answers and explanations to the practice test. Each **chapter** focuses on a skill or set of related skills, such as the chapter about vocabulary in context or the chapter about main idea, summary, and theme. The **practice test** was created to resemble the style, structure, difficulty level, and skills common in actual standardized-achievement tests. The **answers** offer explanations to the questions on the practice test.

Each **chapter** contains the following:

- an introduction that presents and defines the chapter's skill(s)
- a step-by-step explanation of how to apply the chapter's skill(s), demonstrated with an example passage and question
- practice passages about interesting subjects with practice multiple-choice and open-response questions focusing on the chapter's skill(s)
- *Know It All!* tips to assist students in further developing their skills

There will also be cumulative **Brain Boosters** every three chapters to review new skills.

The **practice test** contains the following:

- passages similar in length and difficulty to passages on actual standardized-achievement tests
- multiple-choice and open-ended questions similar in wording and difficulty to questions on actual standardized-achievement tests
- a bubble sheet, similar to bubble sheets on actual standardized-achievement tests, for students to fill in their answers to multiple-choice questions

Explanations following the practice test illustrate the best methods to solve each question.

About The Princeton Review

The Princeton Review is one of the nation's leaders in test preparation. We prepare more than two million students every year with our courses, books, online services, and software programs. We help students around the country on many statewide and national standardized tests in a variety of subjects and grade levels. Additionally, we help students on college entrance exams such as the SAT-I, SAT-II, and ACT. Our strategies and techniques are unique and, most important, successful. Our goal is to reinforce skills that students have been taught in the classroom and to show how to apply these skills to the format and structure of standardized tests.

About Standardized-Achievement Tests

Across the nation, different standardized-achievement tests are being used in different locations to assess students. States choose what tests they want to administer and often districts within the state choose to administer additional tests. Some states administer state-specific tests, which are tests given only in that state and linked to that state's curriculum. Examples of state-specific tests are the Florida Comprehensive Assessment Test (FCAT) and the Massachusetts Comprehensive Assessment System (MCAS). Other states administer national tests, which are tests used in several states in the nation. Examples of some national tests are the Stanford Achievement Test (SAT9), Iowa Test of Basic Skills (ITBS), and Terranova/CTBS (Comprehensive Test of Basic Skills). Some states administer both state-specific tests and national tests.

To find out more information about state-specific tests, go to www.nclb.gov/next/where/statecontacts.html. You can also click on "Assessment Advisor" at k12.princetonreview.com.

Most tests administered to students contain multiple-choice and open-ended questions. Some tests are timed; others are not. Some tests are used to determine if a student can be promoted to the next grade; others are not.

To find out about what test(s) students will take, when the test(s) will be given, if the test is timed, if it affects grade promotion, or other questions, contact your school or your local school district.

None of the tests can assess all of the unique qualities of your student or child. They are intended to show how well students can apply skills they have learned in school in a testing situation.

National tests are not connected to specific state's curricula but have been created to include content that most likely would be taught in your student's grade and subject. Therefore, sometimes a national test will test content that has not been taught in your student's grade or school. National tests show how well a student has done on the test in comparison with how well other students in the nation have done on that test.

Student
Introduction

Student Introduction

About This Book

A *know it all* is someone who loves information and wants to learn new things. A *know it all* is someone who wants to be amazed by what he or she learns. A *know it all* is someone who is excited by the strange and unusual.

Know It All! is an adventure for your mind. *Know It All!* is chock-full of wild, weird, zany, interesting, and unbelievable articles—all of which contain true information!

In addition to feeding your brain all sorts of interesting information, *Know It All!* will give you test-taking tips and standardized-test practice.

By the end of this book, you will have the strongest brain you've ever had! You'll be ready for a Brain Olympics, to become the president of the United Brains of the Universe. You'll be a *know it all*!

Know It All! contains **chapters, Brain Boosters,** and a **practice test.**

Each **chapter**
- defines a skill or group of skills, such as the chapter about vocabulary or the chapter about summary, main idea, and theme
- shows how to use these skills to answer an example question
- provides practice passages and questions like those you may see on standardized tests in school

Each **Brain Booster**
- reviews the skills from the three previous chapters
- includes fun and interesting reading passages

The **practice test**
- provides passages similar to passages on standardized tests
- gives questions similar to questions on standardized tests
- provides a bubble sheet similar to the type on standardized-achievement tests (to help you become an expert at bubble sheets)

You will get answers to the questions in the chapters and Brain Boosters. Also, there will be answers and explanations to the questions in the practice test.

About Standardized-Achievement Tests

Standardized-achievement tests. Who? What? Where? When? Why? How?

You know about them. You've probably taken them. But you might have a few questions about them. If you want to be a *know it all,* it would be good for you to know about standardized-achievement tests.

The words *standardized* and *achievement* describe the word *tests. Standardized* means to compare something with a standard or a level. Standardized tests often use standards that have been decided by your school, district, or state. These standards list the skills you will learn in diffcrent subjects in different grades. *Achievement* means how much good work you can do, a heroic act, or something that took a lot of effort. So *standardized-achievement tests* are tests that check the quality of your work with certain skills. According to these definitions, you can consider yourself an impressive hero for all of your efforts.

To find out the nitty-gritty about any standardized-achievement tests you may take, ask your teachers and/or parents. Here are some questions you might want to ask.

Who?	You!
What?	What kinds of questions will be on the test?
	What kinds of skills will be tested?
Where?	Where will the test happen?
When?	When will the test happen?
	How much time will I have to complete the test?
Why?	What affect will my score have?
How?	How should I be prepared?
	Do I need to bring anything to the test?
	If I don't know the answer to a question, should I guess?

None of the tests can assess your special qualities as a *know it all.* They are meant to show how well you can use the skills that you learned in school on a standardized test.

About the Icons in This Book

This book contains many different small pictures, called icons. The icons tell you about the topics in the articles in the book.

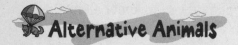 Alternative Animals

Read these passages to learn about animals that you never knew existed and feats that you never knew animals could accomplish. You'll learn about the biggest, smallest, oldest, fastest, and most interesting animals on the planet. You can find these passages in Chapters 1, 6, 9, 12, and Brain Booster #5.

 Hip History

Your goal is to read about some of the coolest stuff in history with some neat historic figures—some of whom aren't much older than you. These passages will help you complete that mission while learning the most interesting stories in history. You can find these passages in Chapter 7 and Brain Booster #1.

 For Your Amusement

You want to play games? Read these passages to learn about cool games, toys, amusement parks, and festivals. You can find these passages in Chapters 2, 8, 10, and 14.

 Extreme Sports

Read these passages to learn about crazy contests, wacky personalities, and incredible feats in the world of sports. You may not have even heard of some of these sports! You can find these passages in Chapters 2 and 5.

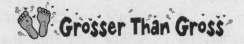 Grosser Than Gross

How gross can you get? Read these passages if you want to learn about really gross things. Be warned: Some of the passages may be so gross that they're downright scary. You can find these passages in Chapters 1, 2, 5, 14, 15, and Brain Booster #3.

 Mad Science

If you read these passages, you'll see science like you've never seen it before. You'll learn about all sorts of interesting science-related stuff. You can find these passages in Chapters 6, 7, 10, 13, and 15.

 Outer Space Oddities

Do you ever wonder what goes on in the universe away from planet Earth? Satisfy your curiosity by reading these passages about weird events that happen in outer-space. You can find these passages in Chapters 13 and 14.

 Explorers and Adventures

Did you ever want to take a journey to learn more about a place? Well, you'll get the chance to do that if you read these passages about explorers and adventurers. You can find these passages in Chapters 4, 5, and Brain Booster #4.

The Entertainment Center

Do you enjoy listening to music or watching television and movies? Here's your chance to read about them! You can find these passages in Chapters 3, 10, 13, and 14.

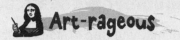 Art-rageous

Are you feeling a bit creative? Read these passages to get an unusual look into art that's all around you: books, drawings, paintings, and much more. You can find these passages in Chapters 3, 6, 11, 12, and Brain Booster #2.

 Bizarre Human Feats

People do some very strange stuff. You can read about some of these incredible-but-true human feats in these passages. You can find these passages in Chapters 3, 4, and 11.

 WILD CARDS

You'll never know what you're going to get with these passages. It's a mixed bag. Anything goes! You can find these passages in Chapters 7, 8, and 9.

Things to Remember When Preparing for Tests

There are lots of things you can do to prepare for standardized-achievement tests. Here are a few examples.

- **Work hard in school all year.** Working hard in school all year is a great way to prepare for tests.

- **Read.** Read everything you can. Reading a lot is a great way to prepare for tests.

- **Work on this book!** This book gives you loads of practice for tests. You've probably heard the phrase "Practice makes perfect." Practice is a great way to prepare for tests.

- **Ask your teachers and/or parents questions about your schoolwork whenever you need to.** Your teachers and your parents can help you with your schoolwork. Asking for help when you need it is a great way to prepare for tests and to become a *know it all.*

- **Ask your teachers and/or parents for information about the tests.** If you have questions about the tests, ask! Knowing what you will have to do is a great way to prepare for tests.

- **Have good dinners and good breakfasts before the tests.** Eating well will fuel your body with energy, and your brain needs energy to think. You want to take a test with all the engines ready in your brain.

- **Get enough sleep before the tests.** Being awake and alert while taking tests is very important. Your body and your mind work best when you've had enough sleep. So get plenty of Zs on the nights before tests!

- **Check your work.** When taking a test, you may end up with extra time. Use this time to check your work; you might spot some mistakes—and improve your score.

- **Stay focused.** You may find that your mind has wandered away from the test once in a while. Don't worry—it happens. Just say to your brain, "Brain, it's great that you are so curious, imaginative, and energetic. But I need to focus on the test now." Your brain will thank you later.

The Chapters

CHAPTER 1
Multiple-Choice and Open-Response Questions

When do some orangutans say "ppppbbbpbpbp"?

What are the little creatures that are chewing on your skin right now?

There are only two main kinds of questions on any standardized test you'll ever take. It's true! Almost every question on a standardized test will be either a **multiple-choice question** or an **open-response question**. It's also true that practice makes perfect—the more you practice these kinds of questions, the better you will do on standardized tests. And your brain will get bigger too, as you start to know it all!

Say "HOORAY" whenever you see a multiple-choice question! These questions usually have four or five answer choices to choose from, and the correct answer is right there on the page! Your job is to pick the correct answer out from the wrong answer choices.

Open-response questions may seem scarier because you can't just pick the answer from a few choices. You have to write your own answer! But be HAPPY because you may get credit for part of your answer—even if the whole answer is not completely right. You will usually answer open-response questions on lines in a test or in an answer book. Sometimes you will answer open-response questions in a graphic organizer. You should answer these questions in complete sentences unless the directions tell you not to.

Some tests contain only multiple-choice questions. Others contain only open-response questions. Still others contain a combination of both types of questions. You will be getting lots of practice in both kinds of questions in this book, starting right now!

So turn the page to start growing your brain! Read the **Know It All** steps for answering multiple-choice and open-response questions, and then read on to practice what you've learned!

The Know It All Steps for Answering Multiple-Choice Questions

Use the **Know It All Approach** for answering multiple-choice questions step-by-step until you find the right answer.

Step 1 — **Read the passage carefully.**

Multiple-choice questions ask about information that you have read in the passages, not about information you may have received from other places. While you read each passage, underline important details or write down important things you think of next to the passage.

Step 2 — **Read the question carefully.**

Figure out exactly what the question is asking by noticing important words like *who, what, when, where,* and *how.* Words such as *not* or *except* usually ask you to find the one answer choice that contains incorrect information.

Step 3 — **Think of the answer in your own words.**

See if you know the answer after reading the question, and say your answer to yourself in your own words.

Step 4 — **Read all of the answer choices.**

Look for the answer choice that is most similar to the answer you came up with in Step 3. Even if you think you have found the correct answer choice right at the beginning, read all of the choices to make sure there isn't a better one.

Step 5 — **For questions that you are unable to answer, try to get rid of incorrect answer choices.**

Even if you can't figure out the correct answer choice, you may be able to find *incorrect answer choices*. For example, you may figure out that an answer choice is incorrect because it is not in the passage or it says something opposite to what is in the passage. Draw a line through answer choices you *know* are incorrect. Then take your best guess from the answer choices that are left.

The Know It All Steps for Answering Open-Response Questions

Use the **Know It All Approach** for answering open-response questions step-by-step until you find the right answer.

Step 1   **Read the passage carefully.**

Open-response questions that come after reading passages ask about information that you have read in the passages, not about information you may have learned from somewhere else. While you read each passage, underline important details or write things down that you think are important. It is okay to write in the space next to the passage.

Step 2   **Read the question carefully.**

It's important to understand exactly what an open-response question is asking by noticing important words such as *who, what, when, where,* and *how.* Some words such as *explain, describe, compare,* and *contrast* tell you what to do in your answer.

Step 3   **Plan your answer.**

As you think about your answer, return to the passage and check your notes or the words you have underlined. Use only information and ideas from the passage when planning your answer.

Step 4   **Write your answer neatly and clearly.**

If the test grader can't read your response, you won't get credit. It's that simple. Be sure to write in complete sentences unless the directions ask for a one-word answer.

Step 5   **Revise.**

After writing your answer, read the question and your answer again. Check to make sure you answered the question correctly, and check your spelling, grammar, and punctuation.

Read the passage about orangutans on the next page. Learn more about answering these questions by reading the sample multiple-choice and open-response questions and the (very clever!) explanations about how to answer them that follow.

Alternative Animals

Goodnight, Orangutan!

Hundreds of thousands of orangutans used to live all over Southeast Asia. Today, because people cut down the forests where orangutans live and sometimes hunt orangutans, the number has gone down to about fifteen thousand. Most of the world's orangutans now live on the islands of Borneo and Sumatra in Indonesia.

Orangutans don't like to hang out with one another too much, especially the adult males. Females and kids like to be mostly with their mothers, brothers, and sisters. Different groups live in different areas and develop habits that other groups might not have.

Some groups of orangutans use tools, such as sticks for scratching themselves, or leaves for carrying spiny fruits. Some groups don't use tools at all. There are some orangutans that say goodnight to one another by blowing raspberries! That's right; they put their lips together and blow to make a long, fart-like noise: "ppppbbbpbpbp!" Can you imagine if you said goodnight like this?

"Night-night, Sis! ppppbbbpbpbp!"

"Goodnight, Dad! ppppbbbpbpbp!"

Orangutans are cool and interesting, with lots of creative habits that they share within their small groups.

▶ When do some orangutans blow raspberries at one another?

- ○ A   when they are about to eat
- ○ B   when they find a tool
- ○ C   when they are going to sleep
- ○ D   when they want to play

Know It All Approach

Step 1 **Read the passage carefully.**

By now you'll have read the passage and maybe made a few notes about orangutans, or you may have underlined important details.

Step 2 **Read the question carefully.**

An important word in this question is *when*. It tells you that you need to find a time that orangutans blow raspberries. This doesn't have to mean a time of day. It can mean a time when something happens, such as dinner.

Step 3 **Think of the answer in your own words.**

See if you know the answer after reading the question. Say your answer to yourself in your own words. For this question, you might think, *Orangutans blow raspberries at one another when they are going to bed.*

Step 4 **Read all of the answer choices.**

Look for the answer choice that is most similar to the answer you came up with in Step 3. The closest answer choice is (C), *when they are going to sleep,* right? Even if you think you have found the correct answer choice, read all of the choices to make sure there isn't a better one.

Step 5 **For questions that you are unable to answer, try to get rid of incorrect answer choices.**

Even if you can't figure out the correct answer choice, you may be able to find *incorrect answer choices.* Look at answer choice (A). Is there anything in the passage about eating? The passage states that some orangutans use leaves for carrying fruit, but the passage never mentions anything about eating. Cross off (A). Some orangutans use tools, but they don't blow raspberries when they find a tool. So, cross off (B). Answer choice (C) is about blowing raspberries when going to sleep, so this might be correct. Take a look at (D) just to be sure. Maybe orangutans blow raspberries at one another when they want to play, but the passage doesn't state this. So, cross off (D). Answer choice (C) is the only one not crossed off, so it must be right!

▶ What are two tools that some orangutans use?

_____

_____

Know It All Approach

Step 1   **Read the passage carefully.**

By now you'll have read the passage carefully and maybe made a few notes about orangutans, or you may have underlined important details.

Step 2   **Read the question carefully.**

What is this question asking? An important word in this question is *what*. Another important word is *two*. These words tell you the question is asking for two examples of tools that orangutans use.

Step 3   **Plan your answer.**

As you think about your answer, return to the passage and check your notes or the words you have underlined. Look at the third paragraph especially. The third paragraph talks about the tools that orangutans use and gives you two examples—sticks for scratching and leaves for carrying spiny fruits.

Step 4   **Write your answer neatly and clearly.**

Sometimes it helps to start your answer with words that are in the question. In this case, you could start with *Two tools that some orangutans use are . . .*

Step 5   **Revise.**

After writing your answer, read the question and your answer again. Check to make sure you answered the question correctly, and check your spelling, grammar, and punctuation.

Below is a response that would get full credit.

Two tools that some orangutans use are sticks for scratching themselves and leaves for carrying spiny fruits.

Grosser Than Gross

Chomp Chomp Yum

Did you know that you have thousands of little critters chewing on your skin? Yup, even right now these dust mites are enjoying a delicious snack of dead skin, chewing on your body, on skin flakes in your bed, on the couch, everywhere! You can't see them because they are so small. About seven thousand dust mites can fit on the face of one dime.

Ninety percent of all dust contains dead skin cells. In fact, every hour, you personally shed about 1.5 million dead skin flakes. Dust mites live on those skin flakes! No wonder your room is so dusty! Dust mites are also the reason why some people are allergic to dust. Whenever you dust, little pieces of the dust mites' poo (yes, poo) and little dust mite skeleton parts are tossed up into the air making you sneeze—ACHOO!

So what do you do about it? Vacuum . . . a LOT. And wash your sheets— billions of those little dust mite buggers could be living in your bed right now.

If dust really grosses you out, you should know it helps create nice sunsets. The dust particles in the sky can catch the rays of the sun and reflect the lovely orange, red, and pink colors of a perfect sunset.

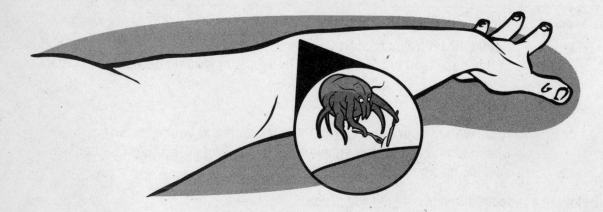

Directions: Answer questions 1–4 based on the passage "Chomp Chomp Yum."

1. What is dust mostly made of?

   ○ A   dust mites
   ○ B   dead skin
   ◉ C   pieces of poo
   ● D   flakes of skeleton

2. What are three places where you might find dust mites?

   on Yourskin, in your bed and every where

3. How many flakes of skin does one person shed per hour?

   ○ A   7 thousand
   ○ B   1 billion
   ● C   1.5 million
   ○ D   90 million

4. According to the article, what is one good thing about dust?

   It creates beutiful sunsets

Subject Review

By now you should be familiar with both multiple-choice and open-response questions.

Remember the steps for answering multiple-choice questions.

Step 1	Read the passage carefully.
Step 2	Read the question carefully.
Step 3	Think of the answer in your own words.
Step 4	Read all of the answer choices.
Step 5	For questions that you are unable to answer, try to get rid of incorrect answer choices.

Remember the steps for answering open-response questions.

Step 1	Read the passage carefully.
Step 2	Read the question carefully.
Step 3	Plan your answer.
Step 4	Write your answer neatly and clearly.
Step 5	Revise.

Now you can answer the questions from the beginning of the chapter.

When do some orangutans say "ppppbbbpbpbp"?
Some orangutans say "ppppbbbpbpbp" when they want to say goodnight to one another.

What are the little creatures that are chewing on your skin right now?
Dust mites chew on the dead skin that is on your body and floating all over the place in the form of dust.

CHAPTER 2
Details

What are the
characteristics of the
Ultimate Snow Fort?

Why would someone
bring a famous trophy to
a party?

How do we know that bugs
are nutritious and
delicious?

The more facts and details you know about one subject, the greater your knowledge about that subject becomes.

When you read a passage, you will learn more about the details of the subject or idea.

Details are bits of information and facts in a passage. You can sometimes find them in a sentence, or sometimes in a word or phrase. Look for the details in this sentence.

> *When Karina's class went hiking at the Grand Canyon, the temperature soared to 100 degrees Fahrenheit, so everyone got very hot and thirsty.*

The details include how the class went *hiking at the Grand Canyon* and that it was *100 degrees Fahrenheit.*

Supporting details are bits of information and facts that help prove, show, or explain ideas in the passage. Supporting details give examples, explanations, and descriptions. Look for the supporting details in this paragraph.

> *It was hot! It was so hot that the flowers drooped in the midday sun and all the desert creatures hid under the rocks for shade. Karina and her classmates hiked through the Grand Canyon and felt very sweaty and very thirsty. Their teacher thought that this might be the hottest day ever; that's how hot it was.*

The supporting details in this paragraph all support the idea that it was hot. The flowers drooping and the creatures hiding show examples of what the heat is doing to the desert environment. Karina and her classmates are described as being very sweaty and thirsty, and this shows that they are hot. The teacher wonders if it was the hottest day on record.

Now read the passage on the next page to learn some wild and wacky details. You'll also learn how to answer test questions about details and supporting details.

For Your Amusement

The Ultimate Snow Festival

Harbin is a city in the northern part of China, near Siberia. It gets very cold there. The winters are so long and cold that the people who live there have a festival every year to make the winter more fun. The festival is called the Ice Lantern Festival. It lasts for several weeks during January and February.

During the Ice Lantern Festival, people build huge castles and buildings out of blocks of ice. These buildings are bigger than any regular snow fort. In fact, they are almost the same size as real buildings! People can walk around in them, climb stairs made out of ice, and look out of the windows. There are also long ice slides and other rides for kids. When people get hungry, they eat frozen fruits on a stick. The fruits are frozen because they are sold outside on the street in the cold!

The festival is called the Ice Lantern Festival because all of the ice buildings have lights buried inside the ice. Each ice building has different, brightly colored lights inside it. When these lights are turned on at night, all of the ice on the buildings sparkles in shades of pink, blue, yellow, green, and purple. It's quite a colorful scene!

The Ice Lantern Festival sure helps people in Harbin stay happy in the winter! Wouldn't you be happy to be able to have so much fun in the snow and the ice?

▶ What detail from the passage tells how the Ice Lantern Festival got its name?

- Ⓐ A   The festival lasts for several weeks in January.
- ○ B   There are ice slides and other fun things to do.
- ○ C   Brightly colored lights make the ice buildings sparkle.
- ○ D   The fruits people eat are frozen and sold on a stick.

Know It All Approach

First read the passage carefully and pay attention to all the important details. Underline the details you think are especially interesting.

Then read the question and all the answer choices carefully. This question asks for a detail from the passage that tells you how the Ice Lantern Festival got its name.

Think of the answer in your own words. Go back to the passage to find the detail that will help you. The sentence from the passage that will help you is the first sentence of the third paragraph. Here is one answer you might think of in your own words.

The Ice Lantern Festival gets its name from all the colored lights inside the ice buildings.

Read **all** of the answer choices again and cross off the ones that don't match your answer. Answer choice (A) does not match because it is about how long the festival is. Cross it off. Answer choice (B) does not match because it is about slides and fun things to do, so you can cross it off too. Answer choice (C) is about brightly colored lights, just like your answer. Answer choice (C) might be correct, but read the last answer choice just to make sure. Nope, answer choice (D) is about the frozen fruit that people eat, and this doesn't match your answer. Cross off answer choice (D).

Your know it all brain has found the correct answer! Answer choice (C) is correct. The Ice Lantern Festival got its name because of all the lights that are in the ice buildings.

 **Extreme Sports**

Who's Got Stanley?

Speaking of ice, do you know what sport gives the Stanley Cup to the national winners? The sport is fast moving, always exciting, and on the ice—it's ice hockey. Every year, the best team in the National Hockey League gets to take the Stanley Cup home. The Stanley Cup is the only trophy of all the major U.S. sports that goes home with the players. During the summer after the hockey finals, the players on the winning team take turns keeping the trophy.

Over the years, players on the winning team have taken this two-foot, eleven-inch-tall trophy on all kinds of wild adventures. Stanley has been to parties, thrown in a pool, invited to Yankee Stadium and the Kremlin, and filled with clams and oysters. The Stanley Cup was even invited to be a guest on the *Late Show with David Letterman*.

Not only can individual players take the trophy home, but the names of all the players and coaches on the winning team are engraved on the base of the cup. No other trophy in professional sports has the names of each player on each winning team listed on it. The Stanley Cup is a true original.

Directions: Answer questions 1 and 2 based on the passage "Who's Got Stanley?"

1. How tall is the Stanley Cup?

   eleven inche's

2. What is one way that the Stanley Cup is different from other trophies in professional sports?

   You have to take turns other sports you get to keep it.

Grosser Than Gross

Waiter! There's a Bug on My Plate!

In many cultures around the world, people like to eat bugs. Yes, bugs. People actually eat creepy, crawly, slimy bugs, stir-fried, boiled, or sometimes raw! It sounds gross, but in fact, some bugs can be quite tasty and are also very good for you!

In Mexico, you can try a dish made from grasshoppers boiled with vegetables, salt, and pepper. In Ghana, West Africa, people love eating termites—either whole or roasted and ground into flour for bread. For thousands of years, people in China have enjoyed a delicious meal of crunchy, roasted cicadas (fat black beetles)—yum! In many Asian countries, people remove the wings from dragonflies and grill the bugs to make a tasty family favorite!

Mealworms can also be a delicious treat. These fat, white baby worms are plump and full of flavor and can be eaten cooked in stews, or even raw.

It's no surprise that so many people like to eat bugs because bugs are so good for you! Most bugs contain almost fifty percent protein, more than twice as much as a steak. You can also eat the whole bug, so there's more "meat" in one bug than in one cow—people don't eat the whole cow! Bugs are also low in fat and carbohydrates.

So the next time someone asks you what you want for dinner, say "How about a yummy baked cricket pie!"

Directions: Answer questions 3–6 about the passage "Waiter! There's a Bug on My Plate!"

3. Which detail from the passage explains why bugs are so nutritious?
   - ○ A   They can be stir-fried, roasted, and grilled.
   - ○ B   In Ghana, they are ground into flour.
   - ◉ C   They have been eaten for thousands of years.
   - ○ D   They have a high percentage of protein.

4. According to the passage, in what country do people like to eat grasshoppers?
   - ○ A   China
   - ○ B   Ghana
   - ◉ C   Mexico
   - ○ D   Canada

5. How do people in Ghana like to eat termites?
   - ◉ A   made into bread
   - ○ B   raw
   - ○ C   added to stews
   - ○ D   de-winged and grilled

6. What is one example from the story of a kind of bug people eat?

   flys people cook flys and worms to eat when
   their reat hungry
   _____

Subject Review

In this lesson, you learned how to pick out the details in a passage. You also learned how to write answers to open-response questions using supporting details. Knowing all about details and supporting details is important for every single standardized test you will take in your life.

Now you know the answers to the questions from the beginning of the lesson.

What are the characteristics of the Ultimate Snow Fort?

Many people think the Ice Festival in Harbin, China has the Ultimate Snow Fort. It is several stories high and full of brightly colored lights. Kids can slide down slides and eat tasty treats while they play there.

Why would someone bring a famous trophy to a party?

Because they can! The Stanley Cup is one of the only trophies in professional sports that goes home with every player on the winning team. The players take the trophy on wild adventures, including going to parties and other events.

How do we know that bugs are nutritious and delicious?

People around the world enjoy eating bugs because they are so good for you. Bugs have lots of protein and can be cooked in many different interesting ways. Sometimes they can even be eaten raw!

CHAPTER 3

Vocabulary in Context

How many languages can bilingual singers sing in?

Where do people talk using a special language of whistles?

Why did Dr. Seuss use only fifty different words when he wrote Green Eggs and Ham?

When you read, you may come upon a word that you don't know. Sometimes you can stop reading and look up the meaning of a new word in the dictionary. When you are taking a test, however, you might not be able to look up new words. But you can still make a good guess at the meaning of a new word.

There is a good way to figure out the meaning of a word you don't know when you can't use a dictionary. You can use clues from the context of the word. The **context** is the part of a passage that surrounds a word that you are trying to understand. Rereading the information in a passage that surrounds a word you don't know can help you understand the new word.

Here is an example. Read the following sentence.

> ***The machine had <u>damaged</u> the floor.***

If you do not know what the word *damaged* means, you might find it hard to make sense of this sentence or to answer questions about it.

Now read the following sentence.

> ***The machine had <u>damaged</u> the floor, leaving long scrapes and marks in the wood.***

If you read the additional context, you should be able to guess the meaning of the word. The context of *damaged* has words like *long scrapes and marks* and *in the wood.* Those words suggest that the machine had hurt or badly marked the floor. So, *damaged* means "badly marked" or "hurt."

On tests, a **vocabulary-in-context** question asks you to figure out the meaning of a word from its context. Read the sample passage and question on the next page to find out more.

 # The Entertainment Center

Twice as Nice

Celine Dion grew up in French-speaking Canada and as a child spoke only in French. When she first started singing as a young girl, she sang only in French. As time went on and Celine started to become famous, she learned English and began to sing songs in English. Now Celine Dion is bilingual, which means she can speak in two languages. If you can communicate in two languages, then you are bilingual too!

▶ What does the word *communicate* mean in the last sentence?
- ○ A grow
- ○ B talk
- ○ C sleep
- ○ D eat

Know It All Approach

Maybe you already know what the word *communicate* means. If not, don't worry. You can use context to figure out its meaning and to find the correct answer choice.

First find the word *communicate* in the passage, and then reread the phrases that surround the word. It also might help you to think about what the passage is about—being able to sing and talk in two languages. The word *communicate* in the last sentence is surrounded by phrases having to do with talking and singing.

Read through each answer choice and replace *communicate* with each word to see if it makes sense in the passage.

"If you can *talk* in two languages, then you are bilingual, too!" is the only sentence that makes sense. Answer choice (B) must be the correct answer!

 Tip You should take your time walking on the path toward knowing it all. Read the articles and questions carefully. Enjoy the time you spend becoming a know it all and learning about cool things like bilingual people!

Whistle While You Work

When you want to talk to friends who live far away, you probably pick up the phone and call them. In some places where telephones are not as common, people use a language of whistles to talk to one another. The island of La Gomera, part of the Canary Islands off the coast of Spain, has a language like this. The island has many mountains, and the villages are so distant that it would take too long to travel from one village to another to talk to friends. So people on the island have learned a language of whistles.

When people on La Gomera need to talk to someone in the next village, they whistle. They whistle so loudly that the sound can be heard up to five miles away. And it's not just one simple sound; it's a complex language that people use to talk about many things. The villagers can talk about the weather and other topics that have an effect on their lives. The whistle language sounds like music and is usually very important communication.

Directions: Answer questions 1–4 about the passage "Whistle While You Work."

1. What does the word *common* mean as it appears at the beginning of the passage?
   - ○ A   easy to find
   - ○ B   simple
   - ○ C   out of the way
   - ● D   unattractive

2. What is the best definition of the word *distant* as it is used in the passage?
   - ○ A   clear
   - ○ B   very tall
   - ✗ C   different
   - ● D   far away

3. What does the word *complex* mean in the following sentence from the passage?

   And it's not just one simple sound; it's a complex language that people use to talk about many things.

   - ○ A   hard to listen to
   - ○ B   not easy
   - ● C   straightforward
   - ○ D   simple to learn

4. Based on how the word *topics* is used in the passage, it probably means
   - ○ A   rainstorms.
   - ○ B   holidays.
   - ● C   subjects.
   - ○ D   friends.

Dr. Seuss, a Word Genius

Dr. Seuss wrote many famous books for children. He wrote *The Cat in the Hat.* He wrote *Hop on Pop.* He wrote *The Lorax* and *Fox in Socks.* Dr. Seuss wrote numerous books for children, far too many to talk about here. Dr. Seuss's books are fun to read because he uses interesting characters. He also uses words that rhyme, like *fish* and *wish,* and *cat* and *hat,* and *hop* and *pop.*

One of Dr. Seuss's most famous books is *Green Eggs and Ham.* Have you read it? It is about a little creature who does not want to eat green eggs and ham no matter how hard Sam-I-Am tries to persuade him to. In the end, he eats the green eggs and ham and thinks they are delicious!

When Dr. Seuss wrote *Green Eggs and Ham* he used only fifty different words. That's not as easy as it sounds. Most books have hundreds and hundreds of words. Dr. Seuss did this because his publisher said that using only fifty different words would be too difficult. Dr. Seuss wanted to show his publisher that he could do it. He wanted to show that it wasn't impossible to write a book using only fifty different words. And that's where *Green Eggs and Ham* came from.

Dr. Seuss will always be remembered for writing interesting stories that are fun for both kids and adults to read.

Directions: Answer questions 5–8 about the passage "Dr. Seuss, a Word Genius."

5. What does the word *numerous* mean as it appears at the beginning of the passage?
   - ○ A few
   - ○ B strange
   - ○ C colorful
   - ○ D many

6. What is the best definition of the word *rhyme* as it is used in the passage?
   - ○ A when words have no meaning
   - ○ B when words have the same sound at the end
   - ○ C when words are not proper to use
   - ○ D when words have many syllables

7. Based on how the word *persuade* is used in the passage, what does it probably mean?
   - ○ A to try to get someone to do something
   - ○ B to cook a dish that no one wants to try
   - ○ C to ignore all the other people in the room
   - ○ D to give someone a high grade on a test

8. What does the word *impossible* mean in the following sentence from the passage?

   He wanted to show that it wasn't impossible to write a book using only fifty different words.

   - ○ A boring
   - ○ B unable to be done
   - ○ C difficult to try
   - ○ D original

Subject Review

Vocabulary is one of the most important parts of reading. The more words you know, the more you will understand of what you read. You can use a dictionary to look up the meanings of words. But you usually can't use a dictionary when you take a test.

When you can't use a dictionary, you can use the context to figure out the meaning of a word. The context is the part of the passage around the word. By paying attention to the phrases that surround new words, you can figure out the meaning of almost any new word.

Now you know the answers to the questions from the beginning of the lesson.

How many languages can bilingual singers sing in?
Bilingual singers can sing in two languages. Celine Dion is a bilingual singer.

Where do people talk using a special language of whistles?
People use a special language of whistles to communicate from village to village on the island of La Gomera in the Canary Islands.

Why did Dr. Seuss use only fifty different words when he wrote Green Eggs and Ham?
Dr. Seuss's publisher said that it would be impossible to write a book using only fifty different words. Dr. Seuss wanted to prove his publisher wrong, so he wrote *Green Eggs and Ham*.

When Presidents Were Young

Perhaps you have heard the story about George Washington as a young boy chopping down a cherry tree. According to the story, when his father asked him about the incident, George said, "I cannot tell a lie," and confessed. This story might not really be true. This might be a story that people made up to talk about how important it is not to tell lies.

There are other stories about some U.S. presidents as young boys that are true, however.

Andrew Jackson

When Andrew Jackson, the seventh president of the United States, was thirteen years old, British soldiers captured him. One day, a British soldier demanded that Jackson polish the soldier's boots. When the boy said "No," the soldier hit him with a sword, giving him a lifelong scar.

Abraham Lincoln

As a young boy, Abraham Lincoln had to work very hard. His mother died when he was nine years old, and his father was uneducated. Lincoln loved to read and write even though he didn't go to school for very long. He would borrow a lot of books to read. He became the sixteenth president of the United States.

Theodore Roosevelt

Theodore Roosevelt loved animals when he was a young boy. When he became the twenty-sixth president of the United States, the White House was full of pets. Roosevelt and his family had a bear, a badger, guinea pigs, snakes, cats, dogs, a rabbit, and a pony. The White House was practically a zoo when Roosevelt was the inhabitant of the house.

So, even though George Washington may not have cut down a cherry tree, many U.S. presidents have interesting tales to tell about their childhoods.

Directions: Answer questions 1–4 about the passage "When Presidents Were Young."

1. Which President borrowed lots of books?
   - ○ A   George Washington
   - ● B   Andrew Jackson
   - ○ C   Abraham Lincoln
   - ○ D   Theodore Roosevelt

2. What happened to Andrew Jackson as a boy?
   - ● A   A British soldier hit him with a sword.
   - ○ B   He was attacked by a bear.
   - ○ C   He chopped down a cherry tree.
   - ○ D   His mother died when he was young.

3. What is the best meaning of the word *tales* as seen in the last sentence of the passage?
   - ○ A   lies
   - ● B   stories
   - ○ C   animals
   - ○ D   scars

4. What does the word *inhabitant* mean in the following sentence from the passage?

   The White House was practically a zoo when Roosevelt was the inhabitant of the house.

   - ○ A   resident
   - ● B   president
   - ○ C   keeper of animals
   - ○ D   painter

CHAPTER 4

Fact and Opinion

Do wormholes exist?

Should people pay attention to what kids invent?

What is a haggis?

The big difference between facts and opinions is that facts can be proven and opinions cannot. People often have different opinions and have conversations, even arguments, about them.

It is important to be able to tell the difference between a fact and an opinion. If you can tell the difference, you will be able to do better on your reading tests. You will also be able to state your opinions more strongly when you speak or write.

A **fact** is a statement that most people accept as true and that can be checked in several places. You can find facts in places like textbooks, encyclopedias, and atlases.

An **opinion** is a statement of a personal judgment or a belief that cannot be proven. An opinion is what a person thinks or feels about a subject. There is no way to tell if an opinion is true. Opinions often use the word "most," "best," "worst," or "should." You can find opinions in places like diaries and newspaper editorials.

> FACT: Andre Agassi has played in many tennis tournaments.

This statement is a fact because it can be proven. You can prove that Agassi played in many tennis tournaments by looking for the information in a book or newspaper. This is a true statement.

> OPINION: Tennis is the greatest game in the world.

This statement is an opinion because it cannot be proven. You might *think* that tennis is the greatest game, but there is no way to prove it. This is an opinion.

Be alert for statements that sound like facts but are actually opinions. For example, imagine that a friend told you, "It is a fact that I am the best basketball player on the team." Your bragging friend is not telling the truth necessarily; he or she is just telling you an opinion.

For more practice, read the passage about wormholes on the next page and answer the sample question that goes with it.

Outer Space Oddities

Wormholes: Fact or Fantasy?

In the movie *Contact,* based on the book with the same name by Carl Sagan, Jodie Foster plays a scientist who is interested in outer space. She is interested mostly in whether there is life on other planets. At one point in the movie, she zips from one place to another by traveling through wormholes. I always thought that black holes were cool, but wormholes are even cooler.

Black holes are old stars with very strong gravitational pulls that suck all the light around into them. Wormholes are tunnels in space that some people think can take you from one place to another very fast. No, they are not holes dug by worms! Some people think there are no such things as wormholes and that it is just a story. I hope wormholes do exist and that I can travel through one someday!

▶ Write one fact and one opinion from the passage about wormholes.

Fact: _____

Opinion: _____

Know It All Approach

This question asks you to find one fact and one opinion from the passage. Read the passage carefully and underline sentences that are good examples of fact and opinion.

The first sentence of the passage is a good example of a fact. You can check the library to see if Carl Sagan wrote a book called *Contact,* and you can rent the movie to check if Jodie Foster is in it. You can write, "Carl Sagan wrote a book called *Contact,*" or "Jodie Foster was an actress in *Contact,*" as your fact.

An example of an opinion is the sentence *I always thought that black holes were cool, but wormholes are even cooler.* Whether or not something is "cool" or "interesting" is a statement of opinion. There are other facts and opinions in the passage too.

Kid Inventors

Sometimes adults don't listen to what kids are saying. The adults are too busy, they say, or have more interesting things to do. But adults really should listen to what kids have to say. Kids can come up with great inventions that can change the world.

In 1873, a fifteen-year-old named Chester Greenwood invented earmuffs. Chester liked to go ice skating in the winter, but his ears would get cold. It's terrible to have cold ears in the winter! First, Chester tried wrapping a scarf around his head, but the scarf kept coming off his ears. Then he made two loops out of wire and asked his grandmother to sew fur on them . . . earmuffs! Chester sold a ton of earmuffs in his life and made a lot of money.

The Popsicle™ was also invented by a kid. When Frank Epperson was eleven years old, he forgot his soda on the porch. It had a stirring stick in it. When it froze, the Episicle was born. That was in 1905. Since then, the Episicle has been renamed the Popsicle™. People love to eat Popsicles™ —they are the best possible summer treat!

So the next time a kid you know is busily inventing something new, pay attention! It could be the world's next big invention.

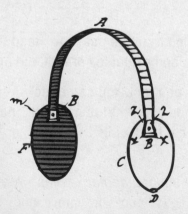

Directions: Answer questions 1–4 about the passage "Kid Inventors."

1. Which of these statements about the passage is a fact?
   - ○ A   This passage is so good, it should win a prize.
   - ○ B   This passage is about two inventions by kids.
   - ○ C   This passage is really quite boring.
   - ○ D   This passage doesn't use enough details.

2. Which of these statements about the passage is an opinion?
   - ○ A   Frank Epperson invented the Popsicle™.
   - ○ B   Earmuffs were invented in the year 1873.
   - ○ C   Greenwood's grandmother helped him make his invention.
   - ○ D   Kids are definitely more interesting than adults realize.

3. Explain how you can tell that the following sentence from the passage is an opinion.

   It's terrible to have cold ears in the winter!

   _____

   _____

4. Is the statement below from the passage a fact or an opinion? Explain how you can tell.

   In 1873, a fifteen-year-old named Chester Greenwood invented earmuffs.

   _____

   _____

   _____

Scottish Delights

Scotland is one of the most interesting countries in the world. It is located in the northern part of Great Britain. The land is covered with green hills and sparkling lakes. The country has a rich history and unique culture. The food in Scotland is particularly interesting, and sometimes very weird.

Scottish people often eat smoked salmon, venison (that's deer meat), and pheasant (a large colorful bird). Scottish people also have a serious sweet tooth—they love cakes and fruits like raspberries, strawberries, and blackberries. Sound good so far?

Well, the haggis, one of Scotland's most traditional dishes, is kind of gross. A haggis is a big lumpy thing, about the size of a football, filled with stuff. The outside of the haggis is a sheep's stomach. The inside is a mixture of grains, vegetables, spices, and sheep parts, usually the heart and other organs. In Scotland, people don't like to waste a single part of their sheep!

The haggis is cut open across the top, scooped out, and served with neeps and tatties. Neeps are what people in Scotland call mashed turnips. Tatties are mashed potatoes.

Another strange dish Scottish people make is black pudding. This is pudding that is made out of the blood of an animal, usually sheep. Blood pudding! It doesn't get much grosser than that. Still, some people think that black pudding is delicious.

Scotland is a beautiful, wild place where people hate to waste anything. So they eat some pretty strange food, such as haggis and black pudding!

Directions: Answer questions 5–8 about the passage "Scottish Delights."

5. Which of these statements from the passage is *not* a fact?

○ A   *The inside is a mixture of grains, vegetables, spices, and sheep parts, usually the heart and other organs.*

○ B   *Neeps are what people in Scotland call mashed turnips.*

○ C   *Scottish people often eat smoked salmon, venison (that's deer meat), and pheasant (a large colorful bird).*

○ D   *Well, the haggis, one of Scotland's most traditional dishes, is kind of gross.*

6. Write two facts from the article.

_____

_____

7. Write two opinions from the article.

_____

_____

8. Would you like to try eating haggis? Why or why not?

_____

_____

_____

_____

Subject Review

So, what's your opinion about this chapter? No matter what your opinion is, it is a fact that you learned some interesting stuff.

You learned the important differences between facts and opinions. The big difference is that facts can be proven and opinions cannot.

Knowing the differences between fact and opinion is useful for more reasons than doing well on tests. It's great for arguments and debates. Hopefully, you can tell when someone states an opinion but says it's a fact.

For example, if a commercial says, "This is the best book that money can buy," you'll know that it's just one person's opinion. You can't believe everything you see or read.

Here's what else you learned in this chapter:

Do wormholes exist?
Some people think that wormholes exist, and some people think that they don't. Wormholes might be tunnels in space that can be traveled through to get from one place to another very quickly.

Should people pay attention to what kids invent?
Of course people should pay attention to what kids invent. Two important inventions, earmuffs and the Popsicle™, were made by kids. The next time a kid invents something, it could change the world. Maybe you will be the inventor!

What is a haggis?
A haggis is a dish popular in Scotland. It's a big sheep stomach stuffed full of vegetables, grains, and sheep organs. Yum!

CHAPTER 5

Main Idea, Summary, and Theme

What can you do about stinky feet?

Why was basketball invented?

How young was Elinor Smith when she became a pilot?

When you are reading a story and someone asks you "What's it about?" what do you tell them?

The summary, main idea, and theme of a reading passage all offer great ways of telling what the passage or story is about.

The **summary** retells the information in a passage using just a few sentences. Here is a summary of the passage about Dr. Seuss that you read in the last chapter.

> Dr. Seuss wrote many books for children. His publisher once said it was too difficult to write a story using only fifty different words. But Dr. Seuss accomplished this feat by writing the story Green Eggs and Ham. Children love reading stories by Dr. Seuss because his stories are so interesting.

The **main idea** is a shorter statement of the most important idea in the passage. Sometimes the title says what the main idea is, but sometimes you have to find the main idea somewhere in the passage. The main idea of the Dr. Seuss passage is "*Dr. Seuss wrote* Green Eggs and Ham *using only fifty words.*"

The **theme** is a more general statement of what a passage is about. Usually the term *theme* refers to a made-up passage, like a story, play, fable, or poem. Themes can be one word, such as *love* or *honesty,* or they can be phrases, such as "Love heals all wounds" or "Honesty always wins over lying." The theme of the Dr. Seuss passage is "Trying something difficult can lead to an interesting result."

Read the passages on the next few pages to learn how to answer test questions about summary, main idea, and theme.

If someone asks you what a passage is about, you can tell them! Read the passage on the next page, and then see how to answer a main idea question, stinky.

Grosser Than Gross

What's That Terrible Smell? It's . . . Your FEET!

Did you know that some bacteria love to eat sweat? And the sweatier your feet are, the more bacteria will show up between your toes, on your soles, and around your heels to eat a delicious dinner. When the bacteria are happily chomping away at your sweat, they are also getting rid of their own wastes, which smell bad. And that's why your feet stink.

What can you do about it, you ask? Well, wear the cleanest socks imaginable, air out your shoes (especially your sweaty gym shoes!) after you wear them, and wear cotton socks. Cotton sucks up your sweat, leaving those hungry bacteria with nothing to eat. The less sweat there is on your feet, the less your feet will smell.

▶ What is the main idea of this passage?

- ○ A Always wear clean, cotton socks.
- ○ B Bacteria are extremely hungry.
- ○ C You can stop the stink of stinky feet.
- ○ D Sweating is a natural part of life.

Know It All Approach

Read the passage very carefully and think about what the main idea might be. Ask yourself the question "What's it about?" Can you put it into your own words? Remember that the main idea tells the most important information in the passage, not just a detail from the passage. Answer choice (A) is a detail, so cross it off. So is (B), so cross it off, too. Check out (C). That one seems more like a main idea because the passage talks about different ways to stop stinky feet. Hold on to (C). Check (D) to be sure. Answer choice (D) contains information that is not even in the passage! Sweating *is* very natural, but if the passage doesn't say so, it cannot be its main idea. Cross off (D). Choice (C) is the winner!

Basketball: The Sport That Almost Wasn't

Winters in New England can be very long and very cold. People can get restless if it's too cold to go outside. That's what happened in the late 1800s at a YMCA in Springfield, Massachusetts.

Dr. James Naismith, a doctor with a degree in physical education, was asked to create a new game that would keep some rowdy kids busy indoors during the winter at the YMCA. Dr. Naismith tried many things, such as adapting soccer and other sports for the indoors, but nothing was working. He almost gave up. But then he thought of a game he played as a child in which he'd throw a ball at a target, and then he thought some more. He came up with thirteen rules and figured out how to play basketball.

Basketball is very popular now. Students can play basketball in school, and professional basketball is seen on TV. The game wasn't always so popular, though. Dr. Naismith didn't really like to brag about it, but he was there when basketball became an Olympic sport in 1936. While he never became wildly famous in his lifetime, Dr. Naismith's name has gone down in history for his important invention: basketball.

Directions: Answer questions 1–4 about the passage "Basketball: The Sport That Almost Wasn't."

1. What is the main idea of the passage?

   ○ A   Basketball has been a famous game for hundreds of years.
   ○ B   The history of basketball is not very interesting.
   ○ C   There are thirteen rules in the game of basketball.
   ○ D   Dr. Naismith worked hard to invent a winter sport.

2. Which proverb best tells the theme of this passage?

   ○ A   Good fences make good neighbors.
   ○ B   If at first you don't succeed, try, try again.
   ○ C   Absence makes the heart grow fonder.
   ○ D   Laughter is the best medicine.

3. Why was basketball invented?

   ○ A   to give young people something to do during the cold-weather season
   ○ B   to create a new sport for the Olympic Games
   ○ C   to keep Dr. Naismith busy during his vacation
   ○ D   to entertain people with a new television show

4. Write a short summary of the passage on the lines below.

   _____

   _____

   _____

   _____

Daredevil Pilot: Catch Her If You Can

In the early days of flight, piloting a plane was much different than it is today. Back then, in the 1910s and the 1920s, airplanes didn't have such fancy controls. Pilots usually sat in an open cockpit in the cold wind. A class of pilots called barnstormers roamed the country, making money by giving rides to people. Barnstormers generally lived a free and easy, if sometimes dangerous, life.

When Elinor Smith was six years old, she took a ride in an old barnstormer plane. After this flight, Elinor knew she wanted to be a pilot. And she was lucky. As Elinor got older, her parents encouraged her to take flying lessons and to get her pilot's license, and she studied very hard. Flying planes at the time was not something women did. Most of the pilots back then were men, but Elinor's mother just kept saying that women can do anything men can do.

At the age of fifteen, Elinor became the youngest woman in the world at that time to fly a flight by herself. At the age of sixteen, she became the youngest person at the time in the United States to get a pilot's license. And as soon as she got her license, she stunned and thrilled the world by accomplishing the feat of flying underneath four of the bridges spanning the East River in New York. No other pilot has ever accomplished this, either before or after Elinor did.

As the years went on, this daredevil pilot accomplished many feats, including breaking endurance records, getting voted as the best female pilot in the country, and being included in the Golden Age of Flight gallery at the Smithsonian Institution's National Air and Space Museum. Elinor charmed and inspired everyone who wondered about the new technology of flight.

Directions: Answer questions 5–8 based on the passage "Daredevil Pilot: Catch Her If You Can."

5. Which of the following words best describes Elinor Smith?
   - ○ A   frustrated
   - ○ B   serious
   - ● C   adventurous
   - ○ D   shy

6. Which of the following statements best expresses the main idea of the passage?
   - ○ A   Elinor Smith's parents disapproved of some of her activities.
   - ○ B   Elinor Smith affected the history of flight.
   - ○ C   Elinor Smith became a pilot because of her family background.
   - ○ D   Elinor Smith was the first person to fly under four East River bridges.

7. Write a summary of the passage.

   _____

   _____

   _____

   _____

   _____

8. What is the theme of the passage?

   _____

   _____

Subject Review

In this chapter, you learned all about how to answer the question "What is the passage about?" Now you know what to say when someone asks you about what you are reading. Here's a review of the terms from this lesson.

A **summary** tells the information in a short passage by using a paragraph or just a few sentences.

The **main idea** is a shorter statement of the most important idea in a passage.

The **theme** is a general statement of what the passage is about.

Your brain is really starting to know it all now. Here's what else you know.

What can you do about stinky feet?

Feet stink when bacteria start to grow in the wet, warm spaces between your toes. To keep your feet from stinking, it helps to keep your feet clean and dry, wear cotton socks, and let your shoes air out after you run around in them.

Why was basketball invented?

Dr. James Naismith invented basketball so that he could keep a group of kids busy in the winter playing a sport. The game caught on quickly and is now one of the most popular winter sports in the world.

How young was Elinor Smith when she became a pilot?

Elinor Smith wanted to become a pilot from a very young age when she took a ride in a plane. She studied very hard and was flying by herself at the age of fifteen. At the age of sixteen, she got her very own pilot's license.

CHAPTER 6

Conclusions and Predictions

Is yawning contagious?

Can animals predict the weather?

Which painter created beautiful scenes one tiny dot at a time?

When you read a passage, you probably think about what you are reading. Perhaps you draw conclusions about what happened in the passage or make predictions about what will happen.

A **conclusion** is a decision you make using clues from the passage. You use information to find a conclusion, much like a detective uses clues to solve a crime. For example, if your cookie has disappeared and you notice crumbs on your sister's face, you might *conclude* that she ate your cookie.

A **prediction** is what you think will happen in the future. You use clues and information in the story to figure out what will happen next. Sometimes a prediction comes true, and sometimes it doesn't. For example, if you are late to school and didn't do your homework, you might *predict* that you will get in trouble.

Here's a very, very short story. What can you conclude from the story, and what can you predict will happen?

> George was hungry, so he asked his babysitter for a snack. The babysitter gave George a banana. George scrunched up his face and frowned, looking a little angry. Then George started to complain in a whiny voice, saying, "I want a cookie! Give me a cookie!"

You might conclude that George doesn't like bananas, and you might predict that his babysitter will give him a cookie. (But maybe she will send him to his room!)

Have you ever wondered why, when one person yawns, everyone else in the room yawns? Read the passage on the next page to find out. Then check out the sample question to see how to answer test questions about conclusions and predictions.

 **Mad Science**

Yawn and the World Yawns With You

Some people believe that people yawn to get more oxygen into their brains. Oxygen helps wake people up. But why do some people yawn at the same time as other people? Is yawning contagious?

To be "contagious" means that something can be passed from one person to another, such as a cold or flu. One theory goes that yawning is contagious in order to bring people together. The theory states that by yawning themselves, other people know how the first yawner feels.

The next time you yawn, see if you feel better when someone else yawns with you.

▶ What is one conclusion you can draw from the passage?

_____

_____

Know It All Approach

This is an open-response question about making a conclusion. Questions like this ask you to tell something that you learned from the passage. When you think about what conclusions you can draw from a passage, ask yourself, "What did I learn from the passage?"

This question asks for one conclusion, not two or three or four (phew!). The passage talks about how people yawn when someone else yawns to make the first yawner feel better. Perhaps you can conclude that yawning is contagious because it makes us feel better when we share an experience with someone else.

What is a prediction that you might make based on the passage? You might predict that the next time you yawn with someone else, you will feel better.

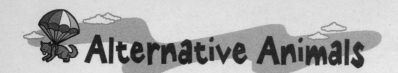

Alternative Animals

Can Animals Predict the Weather?

A farmer and a meteorologist were talking about how to predict the weather. A meteorologist is a scientist who studies weather patterns and can tell us if the weekend will be rainy or sunny.

"One way that I can tell that it is going to rain is when the air pressure is low," said the meteorologist.

"Why go through all the trouble of measuring the air pressure?" asked the farmer. "I can tell that it's going to rain just by looking at the animals."

"Oh, really?" said the meteorologist. "How can this be true? It's not scientific."

"Science, schmience," said the farmer. "All I know is that when my cows lie down in the field, it is sure to rain soon. Also, when the fish in my pond start to jump up out of the water, it's a sure sign that rain is coming. And when the crickets start chirping faster, then it's getting hot."

"Well, I think science can explain *that*." said the meteorologist.

"Oh, yeah? How?" asked the farmer.

"Well, cows might not like the air pressure changes. They could lie down to get more comfortable when it gets rainy. Also, when the air is damp, the bugs in the air might fly a little lower. That means the fish can jump up and eat them."

"I don't know," the farmer said. "All I care about is knowing how to plant my crops," the farmer shrugged.

The meteorologist was just trying to help. "I think the only good way to predict the weather is by using machines to measure the atmosphere," she added.

"Why don't you come to my farm sometime so I can prove to you that the animals do an even better job?" the farmer asked.

"Okay, I will." The meteorologist shook the farmer's hand and promised to visit him on the farm one day.

Directions: Answer questions 1–3 about the passage "Can Animals Predict the Weather?"

1. What conclusion can be made based on the information in the passage?
   - ○ A   Fish get very hungry after it rains.
   - ○ B   Meteorologists are not very friendly.
   - ○ C   There is more than one way to predict the weather.
   - ○ D   The best way to tell if it is going to rain is by watching cows.

2. What is **not** a way the farmer says animals can predict the weather?
   - ○ A   Cows lie down when it is going to rain.
   - ○ B   Fish jump out of the pond when it is going to rain.
   - ○ C   Crickets chirp faster when it is going to be hot.
   - ○ D   Birds hide under the leaves when storms come.

3. What do you predict the scientist and the farmer will do next?

   _____

   _____

   _____

   _____

Dot, Dot, Dot • • •

Often, when artists paint pictures, they brush paint onto paper or a canvas in long strokes. Georges Seurat was a painter who did *not* paint this way. He made paintings out of hundreds of thousands of different-colored dots of paint. He was the first painter to use this method. Try to draw a picture using just dots, and you will find out that it takes a *loooooong* time.

Georges Seurat was born in France in 1859 and was a very good artist at a very young age. The more he painted, the more Seurat became interested in colors. One way to experiment with colors was to make paintings out of many different-colored dots. If you look at these dots from very far away, they seem to blend together to make a lovely picture.

One of Seurat's most famous paintings is *Sunday Afternoon on the Island of La Grande Jatte.* It's a very big painting, so it must have taken him a long time to paint all those dots!

Directions: Answer questions 4–7 based on the passage "Dot, Dot, Dot . . ."

4. What can you conclude about the personality of Georges Seurat based on the information in the passage?
    ○ A   He was very patient.
    ○ B   He was very shy.
    ○ C   He didn't like painting.
    ○ D   He enjoyed the park.

5. What makes Georges Seurat such a famous painter?
    ○ A   His paintings were very simple.
    ○ B   He painted interesting scenes of family life.
    ○ C   His paintings were difficult to understand.
    ○ D   He made amazing paintings using only dots.

6. What is one more thing that you would like to know about Georges Seurat?

    _____

    _____

    _____

7. What do you think happened the first time other people saw Georges Seurat's paintings?

    _____

    _____

    _____

Subject Review

You make predictions and draw conclusions all the time when you are reading a story. Making predictions and drawing conclusions are important parts of reading a passage.

A **conclusion** is a decision you make using clues from the passage.

A **prediction** is what you think will happen in the future.

Did you predict that you also have learned some interesting facts about the world? Well, here they are.

Is yawning contagious?

Yes, it is very common for people to start to yawn when other people are yawning. Some scientists think the reason for this is we feel better when other people are experiencing the same things as we are.

Can animals predict the weather?

Many people believe that animals can predict the weather, or that animal behavior can tell us what the weather will be like. Meteorologists usually think that machines do the best job of predicting the weather. Many people agree with that point of view.

Which painter created beautiful scenes one tiny dot at a time?

Georges Seurat liked to create paintings using many little dots. This was a way that he could experiment with combining different colors. Many people enjoy the paintings of Georges Seurat. While Seurat was the first painter to use tiny dots to paint, he was not the last. The style is called pointillism.

 **Art-rageous**

Photography for a Better Tomorrow

Guatemala is a South American country that struggled through a civil war, which ended in 1996. Most people in Guatemala have very little money. Many of the children have to work to help support their families and can't go to school.

Providing education is a good way to help people in Guatemala improve their lives. That's what one group of photographers and teachers believe. An organization called Fotokids is helping Guatemalan children learn photography and go to school. The program started in 1991. That's when a photographer helped a group of children who lived and worked in the trash dump in Guatemala City. What a terrible job, especially for little kids who should be in school!

Fotokids gives cameras to each child in the program and helps them learn to take pictures. Taking pictures helps children learn about themselves and their environment. It also helps them change their own lives. That's because going to school is a part of the program.

The Guatemalan children have taken pictures that show other people what their lives are like. These pictures have been shown in many cities around the world. It's important to think about people in other places and about how to help them. Photographs help us do this. By taking pictures, the Guatemalan kids can help themselves, their communities, and the world.

Directions: Answer questions 1–4 about the passage "Photography for a Better Tomorrow."

1. Which of the following sentences best states the main idea of the passage?

   ○ A   Guatemala is not a very interesting country to visit.
   ○ B   In some places in the world, children have to work and don't go to school.
   ○ C   Children who learn photography do better in school.
   ○ D   A photography program in Guatemala helps kids improve their lives.

2. Which of the following statements from the passage is an opinion?

   ○ A   *These pictures have been shown in many cities around the world.*
   ○ B   *What a terrible job, especially for little kids who should be in school!*
   ○ C   *Guatemala is a South American country that struggled through a civil war.*
   ○ D   *Fotokids gives cameras to each child in the program and helps them learn to take pictures.*

3. What is one conclusion you can make about the lives of most people in Guatemala?

   _____
   _____

4. Write a short summary of the passage.

   _____
   _____
   _____
   _____
   _____

CHAPTER 7

What and Why Writers Write

Is a passage about a pirate meant to tell you to be a pirate?

Is it true that soap is made from fat, or did the writer just make it up?

Why would anyone want to write about toilet paper?

Writers write in different styles and about different topics. But they usually write in one of the following two main categories.

- **Fiction** writing tells a made-up story. Novels, short stories, and plays are usually fiction. For example, *Tales of a Fourth Grade Nothing* is a novel Judy Blume wrote about a made-up character, who is in fourth grade. It is fiction.

- **Nonfiction** writing shares facts and true information. Reference books, such as dictionaries, encyclopedias, almanacs, and biographies, are nonfiction. For example, *The Encyclopedia Britannica* contains accurate information about many topics. It is nonfiction.

There are several reasons why writers write.

- Some writers want to **entertain readers** with imaginative stories. For example, novels and short stories entertain readers. Most writing meant to entertain is fiction.

- Some writers want **to inform readers** of facts. For example, newspaper articles, history books, and biographies inform readers. Most writing meant to inform is nonfiction.

- Some writers want to **convince readers** using both their imagination and facts. For example, advertisements and opinion articles in the newspaper may try to convince readers.

- Sometimes writers write to inform, entertain, and convince readers all at the same time!

Want to learn about some neat pirates? Read the passage on the next page. Then, complete the sample questions about why a writer might write about pirates.

Ahoy, Matey

When you think of eye patches, hooks for hands, talking parrots, and hunts for gold, what comes to mind? These descriptions probably make you think about pirates. One of the best-known pirates, Cheng I Sao, was the leader of about fifty thousand pirates in the early 1800s. Based on historical records, she didn't have a hook, an eye patch, or any talking parrots—but she did have a love of gold and more than fifteen hundred boats.

Cheng I Sao's group of pirates was known as the Red Flag Fleet. The group stole from ships and Chinese villages. Navy fleets from China, England, and Portugal all tried to stop Cheng I Sao. They couldn't! Eventually, the Chinese government offered Cheng I Sao a deal. If she and the Red Flag Fleet would end their pirating, then the government would not try to punish the pirates. The deal was tempting because if the Red Flag Fleet were ever defeated, Cheng I Sao and all the pirates would be punished by death. As a result of the deal, most of the pirates in the Red Flag Fleet were able to keep their loot as long as they stopped pirating. Cheng I Sao chose to live the rest of her life quietly as a very wealthy woman.

▶ The author of this passage wants to

- ○ A describe what it is like to be robbed by a pirate.
- ○ B share information about Cheng I Sao and the Red Flag Fleet.
- ○ C imagine what Cheng I Sao said to the Chinese government.
- ○ D make you believe that pirates always like parrots that can talk.

Know It All Approach

Read the article carefully. Try to get into it. Did you laugh at any of the words? Underline those words. Underline the words that you think are the most interesting and important.

Carefully read the question and all four answer choices. Only use information from the passage to answer the question—not stuff you learned from other sources.

What about answer choice (A)? Do you think the author wrote the passage to describe what being robbed by a pirate is like? Look back at the passage. The author wrote that the Red Flag Fleet stole from ships and Chinese Villages. But she doesn't describe what this was like. The story is mostly about Cheng I Sao and her fleet. So, answer choice (A) is not correct. Draw a line through answer choice (A).

What about answer choice (B)? Do you think the author wrote the passage to share information about Cheng I Sao and the Red Flag Fleet? The passage is mainly about Cheng I Sao and the Red Flag Fleet. This is probably the correct answer, but check answer choices (C) and (D) just in case.

What about answer choice (C)? Do you think the author wrote the passage to imagine what Cheng I Sao said to the Chinese government? There is information about how the government offered a deal to Cheng I Sao but nothing about what she may have said to the government. So answer choice (C) is not correct. Draw a line through it.

What about answer choice (D)? Do you think the author wrote the passage to make you believe that pirates always like parrots that can talk? The author didn't say that Cheng I Sao or pirates in the Red Flag Fleet liked talking parrots. Therefore, answer choice (D) is not correct. Draw a line through it!

The **Know It All Approach** has helped you find the correct answer—answer choice (B). The author wrote the article to share information about Cheng I Sao and the Red Flag Fleet.

Mad Science

Mystery of Soap

A secret hides in many homes. Yes, the secret is in the soap. There is more to the simple bar of soap than you may know.

Most soaps contain two basic ingredients. The first is fat. Modern soaps are usually made from plant fats such as cocoa butter. But many of the first soaps came from animal fats such as pork or beef. If you lived in the 1800s, you might have made soap from the fats left over from your dinner. That means that if your hands got greasy from eating dinner, you would wash them off using soap made from the dinner! That's pretty wild, right?

The second essential ingredient is lye, which is a dangerous chemical. Even though people use lye in soap, it can burn people's skin. How is this possible? When the lye is mixed with fat, it changes to something else. Together, the lye and fat form soap and glycerin. Glycerin is a natural moisturizer and great for your skin. That means the lye in soap turns from something harmful to something helpful! Consider the Mystery of Soap solved!

Directions: Answer questions 1 and 2 about the passage "Mystery of Soap."

1. What was the author's main purpose for writing the passage?
   - A   to describe plant and animal fat
   - B   to give information about how soap is made
   - C   to compare soap made from animal fat and soap made from plant fat
   - D   to tell about the investigation of a mystery

2. Which of the following would **most likely** contain more information about how to make soap?
   - A   *When Soap Gets in Your Eyes: A Play in Four Acts*
   - B   *Creative Soaps: Using Your Imagination With Soap Making*
   - C   *How to Moisturize Your Skin With Stuff in Your Kitchen*
   - D   *Poems from Around the World Celebrating Suds*

When You've Got to Go

I believe we have ignored the most important invention in modern history—toilet paper. This invention changed the lives of people all over the world.

Using the News

Some people use newspaper to catch their pets' droppings. But people used newspaper on themselves before toilet paper was invented! Perhaps the habit of reading on the toilet started then! Over the years, people used leaves, extra fabric, and pages ripped from books. American settlers used corncobs. Ouch!

Don't Forget to Flush

The first toilet paper was created for the Chinese emperor in the late 1300s. A single piece of this toilet paper was two feet by three feet. That's about the size of a poster you might hang on your wall! The first flushing toilet wasn't invented for another two hundred years. The first packaged toilet paper was invented in the middle of the 1800s. Merchants started selling toiler paper on rolls by about 1890. And by the early 1930s, companies began selling packages of four rolls of toilet paper.

One Small Flush for Man, One Giant Flush for Mankind

Now you can buy toilet paper in different colors or with extra softness. You can buy packages of eight rolls, twenty-four rolls, or more. Pretty soon we may not even need toilet paper! In 1999, Japanese inventors created the first paperless toilet. The paperless toilet takes care of everything. It washes, rinses, and blows dry the person who uses it.

So the next time you have to go, take a moment to be thankful for that soft roll of paper. Only about a hundred years ago, most people didn't have toilet paper. And in a hundred more years, toilet paper might become just another thing for the history books.

Directions: Answer questions 3–5 based on the passage "When You've Got to Go."

3. The author probably divided the article into sections to
   - ○ A   emphasize different groups of details.
   - ○ B   convince readers that the paragraph about toilet paper in the past is more interesting than the paragraph about the paperless toilet.
   - ○ C   list each step in the creation of the first toilet paper in order.
   - ○ D   amuse readers by providing funny titles to each section.

4. Why did the author write the article?
   - ○ A   to convince readers that toilet paper is better than a paperless toilet
   - ○ B   to entertain readers with funny stories about life before the invention of toilet paper
   - ○ C   to help readers understand the history of toilet paper
   - ○ D   to make readers believe that toilet paper is important when training pets

5. Use information from the passage to describe the purpose of the article.

   _____

   _____

   _____

   _____

   _____

Subject Review

Writers write for different reasons. Some authors write to entertain their readers. Others write to inform. And others write to convince their readers. Sometimes a writing selection will do more than one of these things. For example, a magazine article might entertain *and* inform readers.

Don't forget the differences between fiction and nonfiction. They are very important terms to know!

- **Fiction** writing tells a made-up story. Novels, short stories, and plays are usually fiction.
- **Nonfiction** writing shares facts and true information. Reference books, such as dictionaries, encyclopedias, almanacs, and biographies, are nonfiction.

Now that you've read all about the purposes and types of writing, you can answer the questions from the start of the chapter!

Is a passage about a pirate meant to tell you to be a pirate?
No way! The passage is meant to share information about Cheng I Sao and the Red Flag Fleet.

Is it true that soap is made from fat, or did the writer just make it up?
It may sound really weird, but soap is actually made from fat. "Mystery of Soap" is a nonfiction passage. That means it contains true information.

Why would anyone want to write about toilet paper?
Someone, somewhere, sometime, fell in love with the fluffy softness of toilet paper. The author felt strongly enough to write a history about the creation of that papery, lovely stuff!

CHAPTER 8

Comparing and Contrasting

In which state can you find both Cheyenne Frontier Days and Yellowstone National Park?

Why would anyone buy a teddy bear for $171,000?

How can the Velveteen Rabbit become Real?

Comparing and contrasting information in a passage can help you learn what is the same and what is different about the people, places, and ideas in the passage. Many test questions ask you to compare or contrast. Practicing this skill will help you answer those types of test questions.

When you **compare,** you figure out how two things are the same. For example, carrots and celery are both vegetables that are long and thin.

When you **contrast,** you figure out how two things are different. For example, carrots and celery are different colors; carrots are orange and celeries are green.

On a test, open-response compare-and-contrast questions may ask you to write about the similarities or differences between people, places, details, and ideas. Sometimes you may have to write both the similarities *and* the differences. You may even have to compare and contrast two different passages.

 When you answer compare-and-contrast questions, always use information from the passage. Never use information that you learned from somewhere else on a test.

Ready to see some compare-and-contrast questions? Read the following story about fun things to do in Wyoming. Then, read the question that follows the passage.

Wyoming, East and West

The Li family was planning a trip to Wyoming. Wyoming is a large state in the western United States with a very small population. Because the state is so large, the Li family wouldn't be able to see it all. Amy Li wanted to see the Cheyenne Frontier Days, the biggest rodeo in the world. Her brother Jason wanted to see Yellowstone National Park, the largest national park in the country. The Li family had to decide where to go.

"Cheyenne Frontier Days has so much to do," Amy said. "There is a rodeo to watch with steer roping, beautiful horses, and bucking broncos—it's very exciting!"

"There's a lot to do at Yellowstone National Park, too," Jason said. "There are mountains to climb, beautiful geysers that shoot up sprays of hot water, and incredible scenery—it would be very relaxing!"

The Li parents didn't know what to do. Both Cheyenne Frontier Days and Yellowstone National Park would be interesting vacations. They wished they could do both, but the rodeo is in the southeast corner of Wyoming and the park is in the northwest corner, with hundreds of miles in between. There wouldn't be enough time.

The Li parents called hotels in each area and discovered all the hotels were sold out in Cheyenne during Cheyenne Frontier Days. They also found out they could camp at Yellowstone National Park, which would be much cheaper. "Yellowstone National Park it is!" they decided. But it was going to be difficult to break the news to Amy.

The Li parents figured it out. "We decided that Yellowstone is the best vacation for us," they said. "And Amy, you can ride horses in the park. It won't be as exciting as the rodeo, but you can only watch the horses at Cheyenne Frontier Days. You can't ride them."

"Hooray!" said Amy. Amy was happy because riding horses seemed much more exciting than watching other people do it. Jason was happy because he could see the geysers at Yellowstone.

► What is one similarity and one difference between Cheyenne Frontier Days and Yellowstone National Park?

_____

_____

_____

_____

Know It All Approach

Wow! Wyoming sounds like an interesting state. Oh, right, the important thing is to use the **Know It All Approach** to answer the question.

Read the passage and the question carefully. Make sure you know exactly what the question is asking. If you read it too quickly, you might think that it is asking for one similarity *or* one difference. The question asks you to write about *both*—one similarity and one difference.

Go back to the passage to find similarities and differences.

> *Cheyenne Frontier Days: Lots to do. Exciting. No hotel rooms. A rodeo.*

> *Yellowstone National Park: Lots to do. Relaxing. Cheap. Beautiful scenery.*

Then choose one similarity and one difference for your response. Write your answer with complete sentences, and check your work for spelling and grammar mistakes.

Below is a possible answer.

> *A similarity between Cheyenne Frontier Days and Yellowstone National Park is that they are both in Wyoming. A difference is that at Cheyenne Frontier Days you can watch the horses, and at Yellowstone National Park you can ride them yourself.*

A Very Expensive Teddy Bear Versus the Velveteen Rabbit

Here are two passages about stuffed animals. The first passage is about one of the most expensive teddy bears ever. The second passage is about the book *The Velveteen Rabbit* by Margery Williams.

Teddy Girl

Teddy bears come in all shapes and sizes. There are fat bears and thin bears, tall bears and short bears. There are bears with brown fur and bears with yellow or red fur. There are bears who wear shirts, ties, or hats. There are even teddy bears with interesting stories to tell.

Teddy Girl is the name of a bear with a history. This cinnamon-colored bear was once owned by Colonel Bob Henderson, who helped to create Good Bears of the World. That is an organization that sends teddy bears to children in need around the world. When Teddy Girl went for sale, someone bought her for over $171,000! There have been more expensive bears since then, but no teddy bear has a story to tell like Teddy Girl.

The Velveteen Rabbit

The Velveteen Rabbit by Margery Williams is the story about a stuffed bunny rabbit with a spotted brown and white coat, fine whiskers, and pink sateen in his ears. He lived in the nursery with other toys, but he really wanted to be Real. In the following excerpt from the story, the Skin Horse, a stuffed horse animal in the nursery, explains to the Velveteen Rabbit how to become Real.

The Skin Horse had lived longer in the nursery than any of the others. He was so old that his brown coat was bald in patches and showed the seams underneath, and most of the hairs in his tail had been pulled out to string bead necklaces. He was wise, for he had seen a long succession of mechanical toys arrive to boast and swagger, and by-and-by break their mainsprings and pass away, and he knew that they were only toys, and would never turn into anything else. For nursery magic is very strange and wonderful, and only those playthings that are old and wise and experienced like the Skin Horse understand all about it.

"What is REAL?" asked the Rabbit one day, when they were lying side by side near the nursery fender, before Nana came to tidy the room. "Does it mean having things that buzz inside you and a stick-out handle?"

"Real isn't how you are made," said the Skin Horse. "It's a thing that happens to you. When a child loves you for a long, long time, not just to play with, but REALLY loves you, then you become Real."

"Does it hurt?" asked the Rabbit.

"Sometimes," said the Skin Horse, for he was always truthful. "When you are Real you don't mind being hurt."

"Does it happen all at once, like being wound up," he asked, "or bit by bit?"

"It doesn't happen all at once," said the Skin Horse. "You become. It takes a long time. That's why it doesn't happen often to people who break easily, or have sharp edges, or who have to be carefully kept. Generally, by the time you are Real, most of your hair has been loved off, and your eyes drop out and you get loose in your joints and very shabby. But these things don't matter at all, because once you are Real you can't be ugly, except to people who don't understand."

Directions: Answer questions 1–4 based on the passages "Teddy Girl" and "The Velveteen Rabbit."

1. What makes Teddy Girl special?
   ○ A   Teddy Girl has a story to tell.
   ○ B   Teddy Girl is not very expensive.
   ○ C   Teddy Girl is tall and thin with yellow hair.
   ○ D   Teddy Girl was sent to a needy child.

2. According to the excerpt, what makes the Skin Horse different from the Velveteen Rabbit?
   ○ A   The Velveteen Rabbit is talkative.
   ○ B   The Skin Horse is Real.
   ○ C   The Velveteen Rabbit is shabby.
   ○ D   The Skin Horse is not very smart.

3. Name one similarity between Teddy Girl and the Velveteen Rabbit.

   _____

   _____

   _____

4. Would you rather play with Teddy Girl, the Velveteen Rabbit, or the Skin Horse? Explain your choice using details from the passages.

   _____

   _____

   _____

   _____

Subject Review

By now, your brain is full of information about comparing and contrasting.

Remember, when you **compare,** you find similarities. When you **contrast,** you find differences.

With all the comparing and contrasting that goes on in the world, you can probably find similarities and differences between every single thing under the sun. You can practice comparing and contrasting different things in your classroom or home.

In which state can you find both Cheyenne Frontier Days and Yellowstone National Park?
Cheyenne Frontier Days and Yellowstone National Park are both in Wyoming.

Why would anyone buy a teddy bear for over $171,000?
Someone bought Teddy Girl for over $171,000 because Teddy Girl was an interesting bear with an interesting history. Teddy Girl belonged to Colonel Bob Henderson, who helped start the organization Good Bears of the World. That group gives bears to needy children around the world.

How can the Velveteen Rabbit become Real?
According to the Skin Horse, the Velveteen Rabbit can become Real when a person loves him very much. Love will make him Real. If you've never read *The Velveteen Rabbit* by Margery Williams, check it out and get the whole story.

CHAPTER 9

Poetry

Is there such a thing as a purple cow?

What does the autumn have that summer doesn't have?

Do trout go to school and have recess?

If you want to give your brain a good workout, pump it up with some poetry. **Poetry** is full of images of mountains, heroes, love, tears, and everything that makes life interesting. In fact, many poets write about what gives them very strong emotion. Poetry is not always easy to understand, but it's worth it! Plus, you'll have to understand the basics of poetry for your English class or for a reading test.

Here are a few things about poetry you should know.

- Many poems are arranged in **stanzas,** which are groups of lines in a poem. Each stanza in a poem often has the same number of lines, but not always.

- **Meter** is the regular pattern of stressed and unstressed syllables that many poems have. For example, *hick*ory *dick*ory *dock*, the *mouse* ran *up* the *clock*.

- When the endings of words sound the same, it means they **rhyme.** For example, *dock* rhymes with *clock*.

- **Imagery** is language that helps the reader imagine the look, sound, touch, smell, and taste of what is being described. If a poem lets you imagine very clearly how something looks, sounds, tastes, feels, or smells, the poem is probably full of **imagery.**

- **Alliteration** is the repetition of sounds at the beginnings of words. For example, "Sally's sister suddenly slurped soup" shows alliteration because all of the words start with the same sound.

- **Onomatopoeia** is the use of words that imitate actual sounds. "Bang," "Hoot," "Buzz," and "Ouch!" are all examples of onomatopoeia.

- **Personification** describes an object, animal, or idea using human characteristics.

Some of the concepts on this page appear in many kinds of writing. A story might have alliteration in it. Or a newspaper article could use onomatopoeia and imagery.

Alternative Animals

The Purple Cow

(Reflections on a Mythic Beast Who's Quite Remarkable, at Least)
by Gelett Burgess

1 I never saw a Purple Cow;
2 I never hope to See One;
3 But I can Tell you, Anyhow,
4 I'd rather See than Be One.

▶ Which lines of this poem rhyme?
○ A 1 and 2
○ B 2 and 3
○ C 1 and 4
○ D 1 and 3

Know It All Approach

In order to answer this question, you need to know what rhyme means. When words rhyme, it means that they have the same ending sound. In poetry, words at the ends of lines often rhyme. Which words rhyme in this poem? *Cow* rhymes with *Anyhow*, and *See One* rhymes with *Be One*.

Try to find the answer choice that lists two rhyming lines. Answer choice (A) says that *Cow* and *See One* rhyme. Is that true? Nope. Cross off (A). What about answer choice (B)? *See One* and *Anyhow* don't rhyme either, so cross off (B). In answer choice (C), *Cow* and *Be One* don't rhyme, so cross off (C) too. That leaves answer choice (D), *Cow* and *Anyhow*. Those words have the same ending sounds, so answer choice (D) is correct!

Autumn Fires
by Robert Louis Stevenson

1 In the other gardens
2 And all up the vale,
3 From the autumn bonfires
4 See the smoke trail!

5 Pleasant summer over
6 And all the summer flowers,
7 The red fire blazes,
8 The gray smoke towers.

9 Sing a song of seasons!
10 Something bright in all!
11 Flowers in the summer,
12 Fires in the fall!

Directions: Answer questions 1–4 below about the poem "Autumn Fires."

1. How many stanzas are there in the poem?
   ○ A 2
   ○ B 3
   ○ C 4
   ○ D 5

2. Which lines in each stanza of the poem rhyme?
   ○ A 1 and 3
   ○ B 2 and 3
   ○ C 2 and 4
   ○ D 1 and 4

3. Which of the following is used in the poem?
   ○ A onomatopoeia
   ○ B personification
   ○ C alliteration
   ○ D meter

4. Write one example of imagery used in the poem.

   _____

   _____

   _____

Alternative Animals

The Trout
by Amy Lowell

1   Naughty little speckled trout,
2   Can't I coax you to come out?
3   Is it such great fun to play
4   In the water every day?

5   Do you pull the Naiads' hair
6   Hiding in the lilies there?
7   Do you hunt for fishes' eggs,
8   Or watch tadpoles grow their legs?

9   Do the little trouts have school
10   In some deep sun-glinted pool,
11   And in recess play at tag
12   Around that bed of purple flag?

13   I have tried so hard to catch you,
14   Hours and hours I've sat to watch you;
15   But you will never come out,
16   Naughty little speckled trout!

Directions: Answer questions 5–7 about the poem "The Trout."

5. Which line from the poem has an example of alliteration?

    ○ A *Naughty little speckled trout,*
    ○ B *Can't I coax you to come out?*
    ○ C *Is it such great fun to play*
    ○ D *In the water every day?*

6. Which of the following is used in the poem?

    ○ A onomatopoeia
    ○ B personification
    ○ C alliteration
    ○ D rhyme

7. Write a few sentences describing what the poem is about. Describe the scene using some of the imagery in the poem. Don't forget to check your work.

    _____

    _____

    _____

    _____

Subject Review

If you want your brain to really know what all of the terms in this chapter mean, write your own poem using each of them and show your poems to your teacher or another adult.

Stanzas are groups of lines in a poem.

Meter is a regular pattern of stressed syllables.

Words **rhyme** when their endings sound the same.

Rich language can include **imagery.**

Alliteration is the repetition of sounds at the beginnings of words.

Onomatopoeia is the use of language that imitates actual sounds.

Personification describes an object, animal, or idea using human characteristics.

You can even write poems about the answers to these questions, if you want to.

Is there such a thing as a purple cow?

There is probably no such thing as a purple cow. Gelett Burgess wrote a funny poem about how he has never seen a purple cow. He is also not a purple cow himself.

What does the autumn have that summer doesn't have?

In some places, people burn very small fires in the autumn to get rid of the old leaves and dry weeds from the garden. Robert Louis Stevenson wrote a poem about the flowers in the summer (the autumn doesn't have flowers, right?) and the fires in the autumn.

Do trout go to school and have recess?

Trout are fish that are hard to catch, according to Amy Lowell. Because she can't catch them, she wrote a poem in which she wonders about what the trout were doing. She wonders if they go to school and have recess. And while fish sometimes travel in groups called schools, they probably don't actually go to school.

Grosser Than Gross

Eyeball Excitement

All kinds of interesting eyeballs exist in nature. Many animals—such as dogs, cats, mice, or monkeys—have two eyeballs in the front of their faces just like humans do. Other animals have very different kinds of eyeballs. The South African wolf spider has eight eyes, so it can see in every direction at once. And the Brittlestar sea star has little eyeballs all over its body that work together to act as one big eyeball.

The biggest eyeballs in nature belong to the giant squid. Giant squid live deep in the ocean, so people know very little about them. We do know that the eyeballs of giant squids are as big as dinner plates—that's bigger than your head!

The strangest eyeballs belong to frogs. When frogs eat, they shoot out their tongues to grab their meals. It can be a tasty spider, a worm, or a little mouse, and then—*gulp*—they swallow it whole. Sometimes, if they have a hard time swallowing, they can push their eyeballs out of the sockets and into their throats to help them push down the food! Yikes!

Who Are You?

1   A giant squid in the sea
2   with eyeballs as big as eyeballs can be?

3   or

4   A frog that loves a tasty treat
5   with eyeballs that help it eat its meat?

Directions: Answer questions 1–5 about the passage "Eyeball Excitement."

1. What was most likely the author's purpose for writing this passage?

    ○ A   to convince the reader that it is better to be a squid than a frog
    ○ B   to inform the reader about how to conduct scientific experiments
    ○ C   to entertain the reader with interesting facts about nature
    ○ D   to persuade the reader to write a report about frogs

2. How are giant squid eyeballs different from human eyeballs?

    ○ A   Giant squid eyeballs are much larger.
    ○ B   Giant squid eyeballs can move.
    ○ C   Giant squid have two eyeballs.
    ○ D   Giant squid eyeballs can see all around.

3. According to the article, what animal has eight eyeballs?

    ○ A   squid
    ○ B   human
    ○ C   spider
    ○ D   starfish

4. Write one difference between frog eyeballs and human eyeballs.

    _____

    _____

5. What are two words from the poem that rhyme?

    _____

    _____

CHAPTER 10

Simile, Metaphor, and Personification

Do plants like to dance to rock and roll music?

Can the sea talk to us?

What monument is a tribute to the hungry boll weevil?

In Chapter 9, you learned that imagery is a certain kind of language. Imagery helps you imagine the people, places, and objects in a passage. Simile, metaphor, and personification are more types of imagery.

- A **simile** compares two different things using the word *like* or *as*. For example, "The river was as smooth as glass," or "The man stayed up late like an owl."

- A **metaphor** compares two different things without using special words. For example, "The river was glass," or "The man is an owl," are metaphors.

- **Personification** describes an object, animal, or idea using human characteristics. For example, a poem says, "The tree sang a song in the wind." Everyone knows that trees can't actually sing. Singing is a human feature. However, you can imagine that when the wind goes through the leaves of a tree, it might sound like the tree is singing. Saying that a tree sings is using personification.

Similes, metaphors, and personification are often found in poetry, as well as all the other kinds of writing under the sun.

Sometimes plants can be like people, don't you think? Read on to find out what kind of music plants like best.

The Entertainment Center

Rock On, Houseplant

During the 1970s, a professor named Dorothy Retallack decided to do some experiments to find out what kinds of music plants like best. In one experiment, she put the exact same kinds of plants into two different chambers. In one chamber, she played loud rock and roll music. In the other she played more calming music. After several days, she found that the plants in the rock and roll chamber had very small leaves and were stunted. The plants in the other chamber were growing much faster. After several weeks, the plants in the rock and roll chamber were drooping and faded like old lettuce. The other plants were smiling, very green, and facing the speakers to hear the relaxing music.

▶ Which of these phrases from the passage has personification?
- ○ A *In one chamber, she played loud rock and roll music.*
- ○ B *she put the exact same kinds of plants into two different chambers*
- ○ C *the other plants were smiling*
- ○ D *drooping and faded like old lettuce*

Know It All Approach

Read the passage and the question carefully. The question is asking you to find an example of personification from the passage.

Read each answer choice to try to find one that describes something using human characteristics. Answer choices (A) and (B) are pretty basic statements of fact. Cross them off. Answer choice (C) says the plants were smiling. Do plants actually smile? This phrase uses personification to show the plants are happy. Hold on to answer choice (C) and check out (D). The phrase "drooping and faded like old lettuce" is a simile, not personification, so you can cross off (D). The correct answer is (C)!

Young Sea
by Carl Sandburg

1   The sea is never still.
2   It pounds on the shore
3   Restless as a young heart,
4   Hunting.

5   The sea speaks
6   And only the stormy hearts
7   Know what it says:
8   It is the face
9   of a rough mother speaking.

10   The sea is young.
11   One storm cleans all the hoar*
12   And loosens the age of it.
13   I hear it laughing, reckless.

14   They love the sea,
15   Men who ride on it
16   And know they will die
17   Under the salt of it

18   Let only the young come,
19   Says the sea.

20   Let them kiss my face
21   And hear me.
22   I am the last word
23   And I tell
24   Where storms and stars come from.

* **hoar:** mold

Directions: Answer questions 1–3 about the poem "Young Sea."

1. Which line from the poem contains a simile?
   ○ A line 1
   ○ B line 3
   ○ C line 14
   ○ D line 24

2. What do the following lines from the poem show an example of?

   Let only the young come,
   Says the sea.

   ○ A metaphor
   ○ B meter
   ○ C simile
   ● D personification

3. Write one example of a metaphor from the poem.

   _____

   _____

   _____

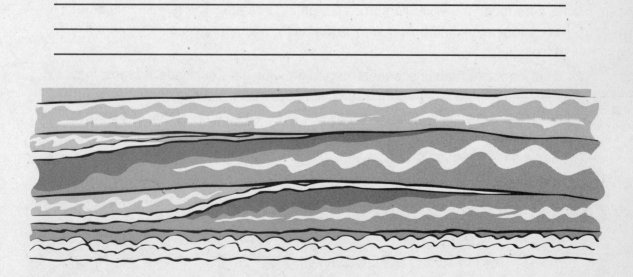

The Great Boll Weevil

If you've ever seen a boll weevil, you know that by itself the tiny bug is pretty harmless. But get a whole group of boll weevils together, and they can eat up entire fields of crops. That can cost farmers millions of dollars!

While most farmers hate boll weevils, there was one group of farmers in Alabama that was helped by the little critters. The boll weevils did such a good thing for these farmers that the farmers created a large statue to honor the bug.

Why? Well, back in the early 1900s, the boll weevil traveled to Alabama from Mexico. At that time, cotton was the main crop grown in Alabama, and boll weevils *love* cotton. So, once they got to the cotton, the boll weevils spread like ants on a pot of spilled honey. The farmers watched this happen and saw their money pack its bags and head out of town. The boll weevils had ruined the farmers' profit.

Not for long! A local businessman was determined not to let this happen. He persuaded a few farmers to start planting peanuts! The farmers became very successful, and their money returned to town, bringing along a bunch of friends.

Once these Alabama farmers started growing different kinds of crops, they made much more money than they would have made growing cotton. They had the boll weevil to thank. And they did: They built a huge statue of a woman holding a big boll weevil high in the sky in Enterprise, Alabama. To this day, people gather around the statue and think about the great boll weevil.

Directions: Answer questions 4–7 about the passage "The Great Boll Weevil."

4. What is the passage mostly about?
   - ○ A the reason why a town would honor a bug
   - ○ B why the boll weevil spread from Mexico
   - ○ C a history of money in the United States
   - ○ D an explanation of why farming is so difficult

5. Which of the following sentences from the passage shows an example of personification?
   - ○ A *To this day, people gather around the statue and think about the great boll weevil.*
   - ○ B *The farmers watched this happen and saw their money pack its bags and head out of town.*
   - ○ C *At that time, cotton was the main crop grown in Alabama, and boll weevils love cotton.*
   - ○ D *He persuaded a few farmers to start planting peanuts!*

6. What type of language does the following statement from the passage contain?

   So, once they got to the cotton, the boll weevils spread like ants on a pot of spilled honey.
   - ○ A onomatopoeia
   - ○ B metaphor
   - ○ C personification
   - ○ D simile

7. Write your own metaphor or simile about the boll weevil.

   _____

   _____

   _____

Subject Review

So now your big brain is full of different ways that writing is made more interesting and creative. Perhaps you'll try some of these things the next time you write a story!

A **simile** makes a comparison and contains the word *like* or *as*.

A **metaphor** does the same thing without using any special words.

Personification describes objects using human characteristics to bring them to life.

Here's what else you know.

Do plants like to dance to rock and roll music?

Actually, plants don't dance at all. There is some evidence, based on experiments by Dorothy Retallack, that plants don't really respond well to rock and roll music, and they might even grow better if they listen to more soothing music.

Can the sea talk to us?

The sea can't *really* talk to us. That's an example of personification. But if you are the poet Carl Sandburg, you might sit by the sea and imagine what the waves would be saying if they could talk.

What monument is a tribute to the hungry boll weevil?

A statue in Enterprise, Alabama, is a tribute to these insects. Boll weevils are little bugs that wiped out cotton crops in the early 1900s. When the cotton crop was gone, the farmers planted other crops that made them a lot more money. So the destructive bugs actually did a good thing!

CHAPTER 11

Point of View and Describing Characters

What Russian writer bought all the copies of one of his works so that he could destroy them?

Who made a working violin out of only matchsticks?

What was Mary Lennox like when she first got to Misselthwaite Manor?

Every person is different, and people are interesting in their own ways. (Some can be a little strange!)

Reading passages are often about interesting people doing interesting things. The people that you read about in a passage are called the **characters.** You read about their actions, ideas, thoughts, and feelings.

The **narrator** of a passage is the character that is actually telling the story. The point of view is *how* the narrator is telling the story.

- The point of view is **first person** if the narrator is part of the story and participates in the action. First-person narrators use the words *I*, *me*, and *we*.

- The point of view is **second person** if the narrator is actually talking to the reader using the word *you*. The second-person point of view is not very common.

- The point of view is **third person** if the narrator is telling the story from the outside and is not a part of the action. Third-person narrators use the words *him*, *her*, *he*, *she*, and *they*.

The **author** is the person who wrote the passage. For example, the author of *The Secret Garden* is Frances Hodgson Burnett.

The author and the narrator are usually different, unless the passage is an autobiography. An **autobiography** is when someone writes about his or her own life. That means the author and narrator are the same.

 Characters are most often human, but they don't have to be. They can be animals, wizards, or even objects.

 **Art-rageous**

Go Go Gogol

Nikolai Gogol was a Russian novelist who lived from 1809 to 1852. One of his best known novels was called *Dead Souls,* which made him very famous. When he was younger, he wrote many poems. One of his poems was called "Hans Küchel garten." A person who reviewed poems in a newspaper thought this poem was horrible and made fun of it. Gogol was so upset that he bought every copy of the poem that he could find in stores. Then he destroyed them all!

▶ From what point of view is the narrator telling the story? Explain your answer.

_____

_____

▶ Write a sentence that describes the main character of the story.

_____

_____

Know It All Approach

These are open-response questions that you might see on a test. It's important to answer them using complete sentences. The first question asks about point of view. Read the passage again and pay attention to the words the author is using. The author is using *he* and *his,* so it is in the third-person point of view.

The second question could be answered in a few different ways. Write a complete sentence using details from the passage to describe the main character of the story. Here are two possible responses.

Gogol was a writer who was upset when people didn't like what he wrote.

Gogol was an interesting person who wrote famous books, but he was always worried that people wouldn't like his work.

 **Art-rageous**

A Man and His Matchsticks

Many years ago, around the 1930s, there was a man named Jack Hall. He was a sailor. Being a sailor was sometimes a boring job without too much to do. He didn't like sitting around on his steam ship during long voyages so he came up with a fun hobby—building stuff out of matchsticks.

It's harder than it seems to build something big out of something so small as little matchsticks. He had to glue hundreds of matchsticks together to make a simple box. It took a long time, but at least it wasn't boring. He practiced a lot, and eventually he could make things like boxes, clocks, and lighthouses. Pretty impressive, huh?

The best thing he ever made out of matchsticks was a real violin. This came after months and months of hard work, but it was worth it! He made a violin and some other instruments that really could be played. And one day, a group of musicians actually played them. And they sounded great!

Directions: Answer questions 1–4 about the passage "A Man and His Matchsticks."

1. What did the narrator of the story think about being a sailor?
    ○ A   He thinks it is exciting.
    ○ B   He thinks it is an important job.
    ○ C   Sailors have too much to do.
    ○ D   He thinks it is sort of boring.

2. Which of the following adjectives best describes Jack Hall?
    ○ A   lazy
    ○ B   creative
    ○ C   shy
    ○ D   experienced

3. Is the story told in the first person or the third person? Explain how you can tell.

    _____

    _____

    _____

4. What is one question you would like to ask Jack Hall if you could?

    _____

    _____

    _____

Bizarre Human Feats

Mary, Mary, Quite Contrary

In the first paragraph of The Secret Garden *by Frances Hodgson Burnett, Mary Lennox is described as the most disagreeable-looking child ever. That is quite an accomplishment!*

When Mary Lennox was sent to Misselthwaite Manor to live with her uncle everybody said she was the most disagreeable-looking child ever seen. It was true, too. She had a little thin face and a little thin body, thin light hair and a sour expression. Her hair was yellow, and her face was yellow because she had been born in India and had always been ill in one way or another. Her father had held a position under the English Government and had always been busy and ill himself, and her mother had been a great beauty who cared only to go to parties and amuse herself with gay people. She had not wanted a little girl at all, and when Mary was born she handed her over to the care of an Ayah, who was made to understand that if she wished to please the Mem Sahib she must keep the child out of sight as much as possible. So when she was a sickly, fretful, ugly little baby she was kept out of the way, and when she became a sickly, fretful, toddling thing she was kept out of the way also. She never remembered seeing familiarly anything but the dark faces of her Ayah and the other native servants, and as they always obeyed her and gave her her own way in everything, because the Mem Sahib would be angry if she was disturbed by her crying, by the time she was six years old she was as tyrannical and selfish a little pig as ever lived. The young English governess who came to teach her to read and write disliked her so much that she gave up her place in three months, and when other governesses came to try to fill it they always went away in a shorter time than the first one. So if Mary had not chosen really to want to know how to read books, she never would have known her letters at all.

Directions: Answer questions 5–8 based on the passage "Mary, Mary, Quite Contrary."

5. What best describes the point of view of this excerpt from *The Secret Garden*?
   - ○ A   It is a story told in the first person.
   - ○ B   It is an autobiography about the author's life.
   - ○ C   The narrator is telling the story in the third person.
   - ○ D   It is a letter written in the second person.

6. According to the passage, what is Mary Lennox like?
   - ○ A   kind
   - ○ B   angry
   - ○ C   smart
   - ○ D   selfish

7. What do you think Mary Lennox feels inside?

   _____

   _____

8. What do you think will happen to Mary Lennox next?

   _____

   _____

Subject Review

In this chapter, you learned all about the interesting people in reading passages. You learned about characters, the narrator, and the author.

- **Characters** perform the actions in a passage.
- The **narrator** tells the actions in the passage.
- The **author** is the person who writes the passage.

You also learned about the specific characters that we asked about at the beginning of the chapter.

What Russian writer bought all the copies of one of his works so that he could destroy them?

Nikolai Gogol was a very good writer, but someone made so much fun of one of his first poems that he bought all the copies and destroyed them.

Who made a working violin out of only matchsticks?

Jack Hall. He was so bored as a sailor that he spent much of his time making stuff out of matchsticks. Eventually, he got so good that he made a playable violin, all out of matchsticks.

What was Mary Lennox like when she first got to Misselthwaite Manor?

Mary Lennox was pretty selfish and horrible at the beginning of *The Secret Garden,* but she gets much nicer later in the book. You'll learn more about Mary in the next chapter; if you want to learn even more, by all means, read the book! It is a page-turner.

CHAPTER 12

Plot, Setting, and Sequence

What is The Secret Garden about, anyway?

Where does The Secret Garden take place?

Who is crying in the hallway?

Every good story has lots of action. This action doesn't have to be as dramatic as a sword fight or a car chase; it can be something like an argument or a problem with friends.

The **plot** of the story is what happens in the story. The plot is a short description of the important action.

The **sequence** of the story is the order of events that happen in the story. Most stories start at the beginning and move forward in time.

The **setting** of a story is the time and place in which a story happens.

Read another excerpt from *The Secret Garden,* by Frances Hodgson Burnett, to learn more about plot, sequence, and setting and about how to answer questions about them.

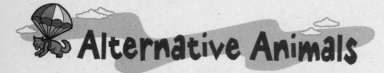

Alternative Animals

Mary's Mice

Now read more from The Secret Garden, *by Frances Hodgson Burnett.*

In all her wanderings through the long corridors and the empty rooms, she had seen nothing alive; but in this room she saw something. Just after she had closed the cabinet door she heard a tiny rustling sound. It made her jump and look around at the sofa by the fireplace, from which it seemed to come. In the corner of the sofa there was a cushion, and in the velvet which covered it there was a hole, and out of the hole peeped a tiny head with a pair of tightened eyes in it.

Mary crept softly across the room to look. The bright eyes belonged to a little gray mouse, and the mouse had eaten a hole into the cushion and made a comfortable nest there. Six baby mice were cuddled up asleep near her. If there was no one else alive in the hundred rooms there were seven mice who did not look lonely at all.

"If they wouldn't be so frightened I would take them back with me," said Mary.

▶ What is the sequence of events in the passage?

_____

_____

_____

▶ What is the setting of the passage?

_____

_____

_____

Know It All Approach

These open-response questions ask about the sequence of events and the setting of the passage. The sequence of events is the order in which things happen in the passage. When you write an answer for this type of question, words such as **first, then,** and **finally** come in handy to show that you understand the order. Here is one possible answer.

First, Mary is walking around the hallways. Second, she hears a noise and jumps. Then, she sees little shiny eyes and finds a gray mouse with a nest. Finally, she sees little mice babies and wishes that she could take them with her.

The second question asks you about where the story takes place. Read the passage carefully. Mary is spending her days wandering around the long hallways and empty rooms of a house. You can answer the question in the following way.

The passage takes place in a room of a house.

 **Art-rageous**

More about Mary

Here is more from The Secret Garden.

She had wandered about long enough to feel too tired to wander any farther, and she turned back. Two or three times she lost her way by turning down the wrong corridor and was obliged to ramble up and down until she found the right one; but at last she reached her own floor again, though she was some distance from her own room and did not know exactly where she was.

"I believe I have taken a wrong turning again," she said, standing still at what seemed the end of a short passage with tapestry on the wall. "I don't know which way to go. How still everything is!"

It was while she was standing here and just after she had said this that the stillness was broken by a sound. It was another cry, but not quite like the one she had heard last night; it was only a short one, a fretful childish whine muffled by passing through walls.

"It's nearer than it was," said Mary, her heart beating rather faster. "And it is crying."

She put her hand accidentally upon the tapestry near her, and then sprang back, feeling quite startled. The tapestry was the covering of a door which fell open and showed her that there was another part of the corridor behind it, and Mrs. Medlock was coming up it with her bunch of keys in her hand and a very cross look on her face. "What are you doing here?" she said, and she took Mary by the arm and pulled her away. "What did I tell you?"

Chapter 12 · Plot, Setting, and Sequence

"I turned round the wrong corner," explained Mary. "I didn't know which way to go and I heard some one crying." She quite hated Mrs. Medlock at the moment, but she hated her more the next.

"You didn't hear anything of the sort," said the housekeeper. "You come along back to your own nursery or I'll box your ears." And she took her by the arm and half pushed, half pulled her up one passage and down another until she pushed her in at the door of her own room.

"Now," she said, "you stay where you're told to stay or you'll find yourself locked up. The master had better get you a governess, same as he said he would. You're one that needs some one to look sharp after you. I've got enough to do."

She went out of the room and slammed the door after her, and Mary went and sat on the earth-rug, pale with rage. She did not cry, but ground her teeth.

"There was some one crying—there was—there was!" she said to herself.

She had heard it twice now, and sometime she would find out. She had found out a great deal this morning. She felt as if she had been on a long journey, and at any rate she had had something to amuse her all the time, and she had played with the ivory elephants and had seen the gray mouse and its babies in their nest in the velvet cushion.

Directions: Answer questions 1–4 about the passage "More about Mary."

1. What is the main setting of this part of the story?
   - ○ A   a long hallway
   - ○ B   a wooded forest
   - ○ C   a dark dining room
   - ○ D   a secret garden

2. Which of these is a correct sequence of events from the excerpt?
   - ○ A   First Mary sits on the rug as she is crying, and then she wanders in the hallway.
   - ○ B   First Mary is found by Mrs. Medlock, and then Mary hears crying.
   - ○ C   First Mary touches a tapestry, and then she finds a door behind it.
   - ○ D   First Mary slams the door, and then she is found by Mrs. Medlock.

3. What event happens before Mary talks to Mrs. Medlock?

   _____

   _____

   _____

4. What is the plot of this part of *The Secret Garden*?

   _____

   _____

   _____

Subject Review

Where, when, and in what order a story takes place are just as important as the characters in the story.

The **plot** is what happens in the story. The plot is a short description of the important action.

The **sequence** of the story is the order of events that happen in the story. A story often starts at the beginning and goes forward in time, but sometimes stories are arranged differently.

The **setting** of a story is the time and place in which it happens.

The answers to these questions show that the plot, setting, and sequence are important to the story.

What is The Secret Garden about, anyway?

The Secret Garden is about a young girl who goes to live with her uncle in an old house. Mary doesn't have much to do, so she explores the house and the gardens outside and, in doing so, meets all kinds of interesting people and makes friends.

Where does The Secret Garden take place?

Parts of *The Secret Garden* take place in a house, and other parts take place in a garden.

Who is crying in the hallway?

Well, you'll have to read the whole book to find out who is crying in the hallway—no secrets will be revealed here! *The Secret Garden* is a lovely story, though, so if you haven't read the whole book yet, give it a try.

Alternative Animals

Kon-Tiki

Thor Heyerdahl is an amazing adventurer. He loves to build boats in the exact same way they were built hundreds of years ago. He once built an Egyptian Papyrus boat called *Tigris,* and two other Egyptian reed boats, the *Ra I* and the *Ra II.* The best boat Thor built by far was the *Kon-Tiki,* and I should know because I took a long trip with him on it.

The *Kon-Tiki* was small and rickety, but Thor and I and four other shipmates managed to sail from Callao in Peru to the island of Raroia in Polynesia. This was important because Thor Heyerdahl once wrote a book called *American Indians in the Pacific,* in which he wrote that people in Polynesia probably came from South America. No one believed him. So he decided to prove it by sailing a route from South America to Polynesia in a boat just like people used a long time ago. The *Kon-Tiki* swam slowly across those waters with a slow but steady determination and a smile on her face!

The *Kon-Tiki* was all crafted from balsa wood and had a small shack on top. The sail was square and billowed out in the wind just fine. The conditions were not that easy for any of us, but Thor had his mission in mind and he wasn't going to fail.

So we sailed about 4,300 miles in seas that were sometimes choppy, sometimes so blue you wanted to jump into them and fly like an eagle. The whole crew ate, slept, and lived together on this teeny boat for 101 days, and despite some hard times, when we reached the end of the journey, we were proud and satisfied, especially Thor Heyerdahl. He spent his whole life proving his theories about different cultures. This trip with us on the *Kon-Tiki* in 1947 was just the beginning.

Directions: Answer questions 1–4 based on the passage "Kon-Tiki."

1. Which of the following is the best description of the passage's point of view?
   - ○ A   It is a story in the present told in the third person.
   - ○ B   It is a story about something in the past told in the first person.
   - ○ C   It is an encyclopedia entry written in the second person.
   - ○ D   It is an autobiography of Thor Heyerdahl.

2. What does the following sentence from the passage show an example of?

   The Kon-Tiki *swam across those waters with slow but steady determination and a smile on her face!*

   - ○ A   metaphor
   - ○ B   simile
   - ○ C   personification
   - ○ D   alliteration

3. Write one simile from the passage.

   _____

4. What is the passage about? Write a short summary on the lines below.

   _____

   _____

   _____

   _____

   _____

CHAPTER 13

Cause and Effect

Why would anyone spend more money than they had to on a house?

Does it rain diamonds on Neptune and Uranus?

Why does ice cream give you a headache?

Most standardized tests have a ton of cause-and-effect questions, and if you know how to answer them you will get a higher score!

A **cause** is the reason for an action or condition. For example, if a football game is cancelled because of rain, the rain is the cause of the cancellation.

An **effect** is a result of an event or condition. For example, the effect of the rain is that the football game is cancelled.

Imagine you are making a model of a volcano in science class. The cause of the lava flow is mixing baking soda with vinegar. The effect is that you will see lots of tiny bubbles, and a chemical reaction will be created. The lava will flow from the top of the volcano.

A single cause doesn't have to end in only a single effect. Many times, one cause can create many effects, much like dropping a pebble in water creates a series of ripples. In fact, almost every event has a cause and effect relationship with another event.

The words *cause* and *effect* can also be used as verbs, so when you see them in a passage as you read, underline them—these verbs probably indicate a cause-and-effect relationship. Sometimes the words *because, so,* and *therefore* also show a cause-and-effect relationship.

To learn more about cause and effect, read the passage on the next page about a really expensive house.

The Entertainment Center

The Tolkien House

Sometimes people will pay more to buy something that used to belong to a famous person. One example is one of J.R.R. Tolkien's old houses.

J.R.R. Tolkien, the author of *The Lord of the Rings,* lived in Oxford, England, in 1918. The house that he lived in was pretty old and historically interesting, but it was just a house, after all. Tolkien became more famous after he died than he was when he was alive, especially because the movies that were made based on *The Lord of the Rings* were so successful.

In the year 2003, the house in Oxford that Tolkien had lived in was for sale. Many people wanted to buy it because it once belonged to the famous author. People fought over the house and so the price went up. Finally, someone bought the house for a lot more than the original price, paying about $1.1 million. The funny thing was that the house didn't even have a kitchen or a heating system! That's a lot to pay for no kitchen.

▶ What caused J.R.R. Tolkien's old house to be so expensive?

_____

Know It All Approach

The question asks you about what caused Tolkien's house to be so expensive. Read the passage carefully. Only use details from the passage when you write your answer.

Some words in the passage will help you. Notice that people wanted to buy the house *because* it belonged to a famous person, and also that people fought over the house and *so* the price went up.

Here is one possible answer.

J.R.R. Tolkien's old house was expensive because he was a famous author and people fought over the house, making the price go up.

Outer Space Oddities

It's Raining Diamonds!

Diamonds are one of the most expensive stones used in jewelry. Even a very small cut diamond can cost thousands of dollars. Diamonds are expensive because they are rare and because they can be very beautiful.

Some scientists believe that the atmospheres of Neptune and Uranus can cause diamonds to form and rain down onto the planets' surfaces. Can you imagine walking through a diamond rainstorm? You would be rich!

Neptune and Uranus have a high amount of methane. Researchers have discovered that methane can turn into diamonds when the methane, which is liquid, is squeezed at a very high pressure and then heated with a laser.

Several scientists wanted to find out for sure, so they did an experiment where they squeezed liquid methane to see if they could make diamond dust. And they could! The effect of their squeezing was that the squeezed methane made black diamond dust when hit with the laser.

One day, perhaps diamonds won't be so rare because space travelers to Neptune and Uranus will come back with diamond rain stuffed into their pockets!

Directions: Answer questions 1–3 about the passage "It's Raining Diamonds!"

1. What do some scientists think is the cause of diamond rain on Neptune and Uranus?
    - ● A   the fact that they are the largest gas planets in the solar system
    - ○ B   the diamond dust made from squeezed liquid methane
    - ○ C   the combination of methane, high heat, and pressure
    - ○ D   the existence of space travelers to these planets

2. In an experiment done by several scientists, what was the effect of squeezing methane?

    _____

    _____

    _____

    _____

3. What would happen if space travelers went to Neptune and Uranus and brought back diamond rain?

    _____

    _____

    _____

    _____

The Dreaded Ice Cream Headache

Have you ever been happily eating ice cream or drinking a cold drink on a hot summer day, when suddenly you get the worst headache in your life? A sharp, frozen-brain feeling all over your skull that lasts a minute or two? Well, it happens to many people every once in a while.

The cause of these mind-numbing headaches is found in the back of the roof of your mouth. There are a bunch of nerves back there that go up into your head. When something very cold hits these nerves on a very hot day, the cold causes the nerves to expand. When nerves in your head expand, ouch! That causes a headache.

No one really knows how to prevent an ice cream headache, but it is possible that these headaches happen mostly in hot weather. So, when it is hot out, be more careful when you eat or drink anything very cold. Don't drink cold liquids too fast, and try warming up your ice cream on your tongue before letting it hit the back of your mouth.

Directions: Answer questions 4–7 about the passage "The Dreaded Ice Cream Headache."

4. According to the article, why do we get ice cream headaches?
- ● A   because cold causes nerves in our head to expand
- ○ B   because the palate is too soft for some temperatures
- ○ C   because ice cream is not very good for us
- ○ D   because in hot weather our brains are more sensitive

5. What kind of weather most likely makes ice cream headaches more common?
- ○ A   cool spring weather
- ● B   hot summer weather
- ○ C   chilly winter weather
- ○ D   warm fall weather

6. According to the passage, if you warm up ice cream on your tongue, what might happen?
- ○ A   The roof of your mouth might freeze.
- ○ B   You might slow down your eating speed.
- ○ C   The ice cream might taste better.
- ● D   You might avoid an ice cream headache.

7. Write one thing you can do to try to stop an ice cream headache before it starts.

   You can wait until its not that cold.

Subject Review

Now you've seen how one event or condition can cause another event to happen. This is cause and effect. Life is made up of connecting causes and effects—and people who like to talk about them. Get used to seeing those words; you'll be seeing them for as long as you are in school, and for the rest of your life.

And now, just what you've been waiting for . . . the answers to the questions from the beginning of the chapter.

Why would anyone spend more money than they had to on a house?

People can get very excited to buy something that a famous person owned. That's what happened with a house that J.R.R. Tolkien lived in a long time ago. People spent a ton of money on that house even though there was no kitchen or heating system—just because Tolkien is so famous today.

Does it rain diamonds on Neptune and Uranus?

Probably. Scientists think that the high levels of methane in the atmospheres of Neptune and Uranus combined with high pressure and heat cause diamonds to form. The diamonds in the atmosphere might actually rain down to the planets' surfaces. Diamonds are very valuable, so maybe one day we'll get to those planets to grab some of the diamonds.

Why does ice cream give you a headache?

When some people eat or drink something very cold on a very hot day, the nerves at the back of their mouth expand and cause a sharp, raging ice cream headache. If people slow down and warm up what they are eating or drinking in the front of their mouth, they may stop a headache before it starts.

CHAPTER 14

Graphic Organizers and Pictures

What makes a roller coaster go loop-di-loop?

Which animal has the weirdest tongue?

Why did it take so long to make a cartoon?

Pictures can help you understand what a reading passage is about by showing some of the action. Some standardized tests will ask you questions about pictures and drawings that go with the reading passages.

Graphic organizers can also help you understand what a reading passage is about. A **graphic organizer** is a table, chart, diagram, or graph that presents information that goes with, or comes from, a passage. On standardized tests, you might see information presented in a graphic organizer, and you might be asked to fill in missing information in a graphic organizer to answer a question.

Below is an example of a Venn diagram. A **Venn diagram** is a way to present information about two things and show what is the same about them and what is different. The information in the center part, where the circles overlap, is the same. The information in the other parts of the circles is what is different.

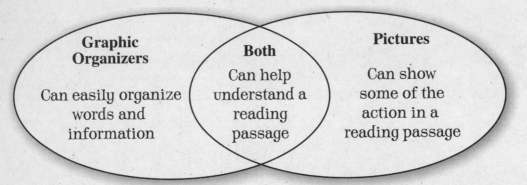

Graphic Organizers

Can easily organize words and information

Both

Can help understand a reading passage

Pictures

Can show some of the action in a reading passage

Read about roller coasters on the next page to learn more about graphic organizers and pictures.

For Your Amusement

Loop-di-Loop

A loop on a roller coaster is not a completely round circle. If the loop were a round circle, the roller coaster wouldn't be able to get around it— the car would be going so fast when going up that the passengers would be squashed in their seats, and then would slow down so much at the top that the passengers could fall out. Yikes! Instead of a round circle, the loops on a roller coaster are shaped like upside-down teardrops—this shape makes it possible for the speed of the roller-coaster car to be the same all the way around the loop. It's all in the physics, but it works!

▶ Complete the information in the chart below about roller coaster loops.

Circle-Shaped Loop	Teardrop-Shaped Loop
Roller coaster travels at different speed	_____ _____ _____

Know It All Approach

This passage and question about roller coasters shows an example of both pictures and graphic organizers. The picture of a teardrop-shaped roller coaster loop helps the reader understand what this shape looks like.

The question also needs to be answered in a graphic organizer. This graphic organizer is a table. Usually a table has titles and then information about each title item. The information under the titles is usually similar for each item. In this case, the titles are "Teardrop-Shaped Loop" and "Circle-Shaped Loop." The information under "Circle-Shaped Loop" is "Roller coaster travels at different speeds." You need to provide similar information about the "Teardrop-Shaped Loop." The information is about the speed of the roller coaster in each type of loop. You know from the passage that roller coasters going around a teardrop-shaped loop travel at the same speed all the way around. You can write "Roller coaster travels at the same speed" in the "Teardrop-Shaped Loop" column of the table.

Grosser Than Gross

Lickety Split

ANIMAL	WHAT IS IT?	TONGUE LENGTH	INTERESTING TONGUE FACTS
Chameleon	A lizard with lumpy skin that changes color to hide in its environment	Its tongue is as long as its body!	The chameleon can shoot out its sticky tongue, which has powerful muscles, to grab and pull in food.
Giant Pangolin	A strange 6-foot-long scaly beast that rolls up into a ball to protect itself	Its tongue is around two feet long!	The long tongue is attached to the Pangolin's hip bones. The sticky tongue is used to pick up ants and termites.
Australian Numbat	A small furry creature that lives in Australia	Pretty long, and very thin.	The Numbat can use its thin tongue to reach into termite nests— eating up to 10,000 termites a day.
German girl	A German schoolgirl named Annika Irmler	Her tongue is seven centimeters long—one of the longest human tongues on record.	Annika was in the *Guinness Book of Records* for the world's longest tongue. She likes to eat ice cream (not termites!).

Directions: Answer questions 1–5 based on the chart "Lickety Split."

1. What is the purpose of the chart?
   - ○ A   to prove that longer tongues are better
   - ○ B   to compare information about animal tongues
   - ○ C   to show what kinds of food animals eat
   - ○ D   to find a link between the name of an animal and its food

2. Which animal has a tongue that is as long as its body?
   - ○ A   chameleon
   - ○ B   giant pangolin
   - ○ C   Australian numbat
   - ○ D   German girl

3. What is interesting about the tongue of the giant pangolin?
   - ○ A   It is longer than the pangolin's body.
   - ○ B   It is the longest one on record.
   - ○ C   It is very thin and sticky.
   - ○ D   It is attached to the pangolin's hipbones.

4. Write one similarity between the Australian numbat and the giant pangolin.

   _____

   _____

5. Write one interesting fact about Annika Irmler.

   _____

   _____

Cartoon Madness

At the beginning of the 1900s, when people first began to draw cartoons, twenty-four pictures had to be drawn for every second of film. That means that a sixty-second cartoon needed 1,440 drawings! Each and every cartoon took a long time to create. Then, in 1914, the animation cell was invented. This cell made it possible for fewer drawings to be made for each cartoon. After the cell was invented, cartoons took off.

The first cartoon to combine sound with pictures was a Mickey Mouse cartoon called *Steamboat Willie.* This cartoon came out in 1928 and was in black and white. Then, in the late 1930s, the Technicolor process was invented, bringing cartoons to life. The golden age of cartoons was soon to follow. From the 1930s to the 1950s many cartoons were created by Disney and other studios. Donald Duck, Bugs Bunny, and Huckleberry Hound were all born. It was a great time for cartoons, and many that were created then are still watched today.

The Flintstones, which premiered in 1960, was the first successful cartoon that was on during prime time. It was about a family living in prehistoric times with a dinosaur as a pet. *The Simpsons* is another popular cartoon that is seen in prime time. It might be the longest-running cartoon on TV. *The Simpsons* began in 1989 and, as of 2003, is still on the air.

Cartoons have come a long way since the early days when one second of film needed twenty-four drawings. In fact, the technology is always changing, and these days many cartoons are being created on computers, without "drawings" at all. It will be interesting to see what the future of cartoons will be like.

Directions: Answer question 6 based on the passage "Cartoon Madness."

6. Fill in the graphic organizer with information from the passage.

The History of Cartoons

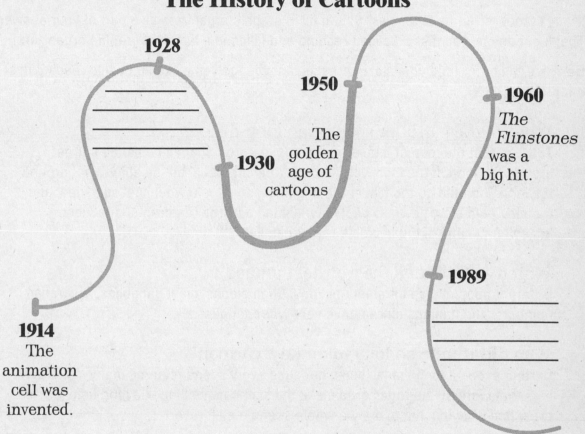

1928
_____
_____
_____

1930

1950
The golden age of cartoons

1960
The Flinstones was a big hit.

1914
The animation cell was invented.

1989
_____
_____
_____
_____

Subject Review

Pictures and graphic organizers help the reader better understand the information in a passage. Graphic organizers can be charts, tables, or graphs.

Many standardized tests also ask you to fill in graphic organizers as a part of your answer. Thank goodness, you just practiced reading and filling in a bunch of graphic organizers!

Here are the other little tidbits of interesting knowledge you picked up while reading this chapter.

What makes a roller coaster go loop-di-loop?

The fact that the loop of a roller coaster is teardrop-shaped helps the car get around the loop. If the loop were a circle, the car would not be able to get around the loop. It would go too fast at the beginning so people would get squished, and then it would slow down so people would fall out. The teardrop-shaped loop doesn't have any of these problems, thankfully.

Which animal has the weirdest tongue?

Different people have different opinions. Chameleons, giant pangolins, Australian numbats, and humans all can have very weird tongues.

Why did it take so long to make a cartoon?

Cartoons took a long time to make because every scene required many still drawings that were all put together to make the scene move. It took a long time just to draw one drawing, but to draw a whole scene took forever!

CHAPTER 15

Finding Out More

How do you get an innie or an outie?

What are hydrothermal vents and what are the squiggly things that grow there?

How deep can a hole be dug?

ooray! You've made it to the last chapter, and your know it all brain should be almost full. Well, if you want to fill it up to the top, you should know about all of the resources you can use to find even more interesting information. A **resource** is a place where you can find information. Different resources are useful for different reasons.

- A **dictionary** is a book that lists words in alphabetical order and tells what they mean.

- A **thesaurus** lists the synonyms and antonyms of words, which are arranged either in alphabetical order or by category.

- An **encyclopedia** has more thorough information on a wide range of topics, arranged alphabetically or by category.

- A **magazine** is published regularly, often once a month, and contains stories, articles, pictures, and other entertaining or informative passages.

- A **newspaper** is published regularly, often every day or once a week, and contains information about current events.

- An **atlas** is a collection of maps.

- An **almanac** is a book listing various facts and is published regularly, usually once a year. Some almanacs have weather and tide predictions. Some list facts like how many people are in the population or what events happened in the year before.

The standardized tests you will take may ask you questions about each of these resources, so it makes sense to memorize what the resources are about. If you have any of these resources at home or in school, practice using them to find out wacky facts to impress your friends.

Read the passage about belly buttons on the next page to learn more about answering questions about resources.

Mad Science

Innie or Outie?

What makes an innie an innie and an outie an outie? When a baby is born, the umbilical cord is cut and the scar that remains becomes the baby's belly button. The umbilical cord is usually cut a few inches away from the baby's body and then just dries up and falls off. Most belly buttons are innies, which is the way the scar heals, leaving a little hole in the baby's belly. Sometimes the scar heals differently, and the muscles around the umbilical cord squeeze a little bit of it to make it stick out, creating an outie. Do you have an innie or an outie?

▶ Which of the following resources might explain what umbilical cords are?
- ○ A atlas
- ○ B almanac
- ○ C thesaurus
- ○ D encyclopedia

Know It All Approach

To find out if you have an innie or an outie, all you have to do is look down at your belly button. To find out more about what umbilical cords are, you would need to do a little bit more research.

The answer choices for this question each give you one type of resource. Read them all before answering. You'd look at an atlas to find out where a place is on a map. An atlas wouldn't tell you anything about umbilical cords. Cross off (A). An almanac gives you all kinds of information about the weather, but nothing about umbilical cords, so cross off (B). A thesaurus might give you words that mean the same thing as umbilical cord, but it won't tell you any more about what it is. Cross off (C), too. Answer choice (D) is most likely the correct answer, but read it just to be sure. An encyclopedia is a great place to find out what umbilical cords are!

Grosser Than Gross

Party at the Hydrothermal Vent

Have you heard the expression "There is more to most people than meets the eye"? This means that people may look a certain way on the outside but be very different on the inside (it's the inside that counts, of course). Well, Earth is like this, too. From space, Earth looks like a smooth blue ball. But there's more to Earth than meets the eye—there's a lot going on under the surface of the land and the oceans that we can't see. Of course, people like a good mystery, so efforts are being made all the time to understand the "inside" of Earth.

The oceans of Earth are deep and full of life. The deeper you go, the weirder the life is. At the deepest, blackest part of the ocean, you can find blind fish that glow green with phosphorescence. You can see huge toothy eels, and big-eyeballed giant squid loom out of the dark, deep, colorful plants swaying at the ocean's floor.

By far the weirdest and most rocking party of sea creatures goes on around hydrothermal (Hi-dro-THER-mal) vents.

Hydrothermal vents are a little bit like underwater geysers. Geysers are natural hot springs that send a column of water and steam into the air from time to time. Hydrothermal vents form on the ocean floor at places where Earth's crust is spreading apart in rifts.

When the crust is splitting, hot rocks come up from the rifts and cool to form new oceanic crust. When the rocks come up, cold seawater seeps down into the cracks, only to be heated to an incredibly hot temperature (which can be more than 700 degrees Fahrenheit) and shot back up again. The hydrothermal vents are shooting this hot water into the very cold ocean. The vents become hot, black, billowy clouds of minerals shooting up from the ocean floor.

Because of the heat and the minerals created by hydrothermal vents, all kinds of weird sea creatures like to hang out there. Enormous clams can be found nearby, and huge red-gilled worms sway back and forth near the vents. Combined with long-necked barnacles scattered around and other growing and swimming things, the underwater scene around hydrothermal vents looks sort of like another planet.

Scientists have worked pretty hard to explore the ocean floor and take pictures of hydrothermal vents to show us what life looks like there. But knowing how people love a good mystery, scientists haven't stopped their research. They are digging holes in the ocean floor to find out what goes on *under* the ocean too. In 1995, a thirteen-thousand-foot hole was dug under seven thousand feet of ocean. This makes for a hole that is 3.8 miles below sea level. That's one very deep hole. The core samples that come out of this hole will help scientists study Earth's climate history, among other things.

So the next time you think Earth is just a pretty blue ball, think about all the complicated activity that is going on under its surface.

Directions: Answer questions 1–6 about the passage "Party at the Hydrothermal Vent."

1. What resource could you use to find out the meaning of the word *phosphorescence*?
   - ○ A thesaurus
   - ○ B almanac
   - ○ C atlas
   - ○ D dictionary

2. If you wanted to look at some pictures of hydrothermal vents, what resource would you check?
   - ○ A thesaurus
   - ○ B almanac
   - ○ C encyclopedia
   - ○ D dictionary

3. Scientists are looking at core samples to study Earth's climate. What other resource has been used to find information about the weather?
   - ○ A thesaurus
   - ○ B almanac
   - ○ C encyclopedia
   - ○ D dictionary

4. What does the author of this passage compare Earth to?
   - ○ A a hydrothermal vent
   - ○ B people
   - ○ C a big clam
   - ○ D a deep hole

Know It All! Elementary School Reading

5. What is the main idea of the passage? Write a summary below using information from the passage.

_____

_____

_____

_____

6. If you wanted to find out if any holes have been dug deeper than the one dug in 1995, how would you research this project? What sources could you use? Explain the process you would use in complete sentences below.

_____

_____

_____

_____

Subject Review

Now that you know it all, you know that there is always something new to learn. There are a number of resources that you can use to increase your knowledge and grow your brain.

- A **dictionary** is a book that lists words in alphabetical order and tells what they mean.

- A **thesaurus** lists the synonyms and antonyms of words, which are arranged either in alphabetical order or by category.

- An **encyclopedia** has more thorough information on a wide range of topics, arranged alphabetically or by category.

- A **magazine** is published regularly, often once a month, and contains stories, articles, pictures, and other fun or informative passages.

- A **newspaper** is published regularly, often every day or once a week, and contains information about current events.

- An **atlas** is a collection of maps.

- An **almanac** is a book listing various facts and is published regularly, usually once a year.

Do you know enough to answer the questions at the beginning of the chapter?

How do you get an innie or an outie?
Look down at your bellybutton. That's how to find out if you have an innie or an outie. Most people have innies, which are formed when the umbilical cord falls off. If you have an outie, that means that a little bit of skin was pinched in there and squeezed so it sticks out.

What are hydrothermal vents and what are the squiggly things that grow there?
Hydrothermal vents are shooting black towers of hot water that come out of rifts in the ocean floor. All kinds of creatures like to party there—giant clams, worms, and strange glowing fish.

How deep can a hole be dug?
Well, one hole that was dug in 1995 goes 3.8 miles below sea level. There are many more miles to go before the hole comes out the other side of Earth, but in the meantime, we will learn all kinds of interesting things from core samples taken out of this hole.

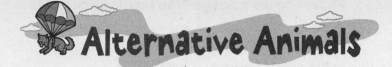

Alternative Animals

The Biggest Brain on the Planet

The biggest brain on Earth is yours you say?

Well, the human brain is the most complex brain on Earth, and we can do more with it than any other creature can do with its brain. But it is not our brain that is the largest. The largest brain belongs to the sperm whale.

A sperm whale's brain is the biggest brain on Earth. This brain can weigh more than seventeen pounds (compared with the human brain, which weighs around three pounds)! The sperm whale's brain is actually pretty complex even though it is not quite as complex as ours.

The sperm whale and other whales can not turn parts of their brains off for sleeping like humans can. If whales fall asleep, they might drown because they have to *think* to *breathe*. Humans can breathe unconsciously, which means without thinking about it.

So what do whales do? They seem to have the ability to turn off one-half of their brain at a time. Then they can rest while floating around in the ocean without actually sleeping. You know a whale is resting when it has one eye closed; that means one-half of its brain is asleep.

Brains of every shape and size are pretty remarkable, aren't they?

Directions: Answer questions 1–4 based on the passage "The Biggest Brain on the Planet."

1. Add the missing information to the graphic organizer below.

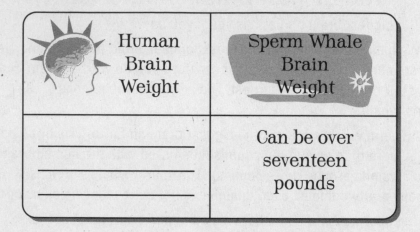

Human Brain Weight	Sperm Whale Brain Weight
_____ _____ _____	Can be over seventeen pounds

2. What resource might you use to find out what the smallest brain on Earth is?
    ○ A   thesaurus
    ○ B   encyclopedia
    ○ C   atlas
    ○ D   dictionary

3. In which of the following resources would the passage most likely be found?
    ○ A   magazine
    ○ B   almanac
    ○ C   dictionary
    ○ D   thesaurus

4. According to the passage, why do whales sleep with one eye closed?

    _____

    _____

    _____

Chapter Answer Key

Chapter 1: Multiple-Choice and Open-Response Questions
1. B
2. You can find dust mites on your body, in your bed, and on the couch.
3. C
4. Dust is good because when it floats in the atmosphere, it creates beautiful sunsets.

Chapter 2: Details
1. The Stanley Cup is two feet and eleven inches tall.
2. The Stanley Cup is different from other trophies because people get to take it home.
(or) The Stanley Cup is different from other trophies because it has the names of all the players engraved on it.
3. D
4. C
5. A
6. People in Mexico eat grasshoppers.
(or) People in Ghana, West Africa, eat termites.
(or) People in China eat cicadas.

Chapter 3: Vocabulary in Context
1. A
2. D
3. B
4. C
5. D
6. B
7. A
8. B

Brain Booster #1
1. C
2. A
3. B
4. A

Chapter 4: Fact and Opinion

1. B
2. D
3. This sentence is an opinion because it is the way one person feels. Some people might like to have cold ears in the winter, or may not mind as much.
4. This statement is a fact. I know this because I can look up this information in another place and it will be the same.
5. D
6. The outside of a haggis is a sheep's stomach.
   Tatties are mashed potatoes.
7. Haggis is kind of gross.
   Scotland is a beautiful, wild place.
(or) Scotland is one of the most interesting countries in the world.
8. Answers may vary according to personal opinion but should contain details from the article.

Chapter 5: Main Idea, Summary, and Theme

1. D
2. B
3. A
4. Dr. Naismith was asked to make a sport that could be played during the winter. He thought and thought and eventually made up basketball, which is now a very popular indoor sport.
5. C
6. B
7. Elinor Smith always wanted to be a pilot. She took classes and got her license when she was very young. She also accomplished many feats, such as flying under the bridges of New York's East River.
8. The theme of the passage is that when you try hard, you can succeed.

Chapter 6: Conclusions and Predictions

1. C
2. D
3. The scientist will probably go to the farmer's farm to learn about how animals can predict the weather.
4. A
5. D
6. Answers may vary but should say something about Georges Seurat.
7. This is a matter of speculation. Perhaps when people saw the first paintings of Georges Seurat, they were amazed.

Brain Booster #2

1. D
2. B
3. Life for people in Guatemala can be a lot of work, and many people don't have much money.
4. A group of kids in Guatemala are learning how to take pictures and are going to school. Their pictures can show people what life is like in that country.

Chapter 7: What and Why Writers Write

1. B
2. B
3. A
4. C
5 Answers will vary but should contain details from the article.

Chapter 8: Comparing and Contrasting

1. A
2. B
3. Teddy Girl and the Velveteen Rabbit were both loved by their owners.
4. This is an opinion, but details from the passage should be used in the answer.

Chapter 9: Poetry

1. B
2. C
3. D
4. "See the smoke trail!" is an example of imagery.
5. B
6. D
7. This poem is about a trout. The author of the poem wonders what a trout's life is like—do the trout go to school? Do the trout play tag in a sunny pool?

Brain Booster #3

1. C
2. A
3. C
4. Frog eyeballs can drop into a frog's throat to help swallow food, and human eyeballs cannot.
5. *Sea* and *be* rhyme.
(or) *Treat* and *meat* rhyme.

Chapter 10: Simile, Metaphor, and Personification

1. B
2. D
3. The sea is the face of a rough mother speaking.
4. A
5. B
6. D
7. Answers will vary but should make a comparison about a boll weevil using a metaphor or a simile.

Chapter 11: Point of View and Describing Characters

1. D
2. B
3. This story is told in the third person. I can tell because the word *he* is used.
4. Answers will vary according to individual interest about Jack Hall.
5. C
6. D
7. Answers may vary. Here is one possible answer: I think Mary Lennox is angry because no one pays attention to her.
8. Answers will vary based on personal opinion. Here is one possible answer: I hope someone will help Mary Lennox and take care of her.

Chapter 12: Plot, Setting, and Sequence

1. A
2. C
3. Mary is exploring the hallway and hears someone crying.
4. The plot is that Mary is looking around the house and hears someone crying. Mrs. Medlock finds Mary in the hallway and gets angry and tells her to go to her room. Mary is so upset that she sits on the floor and grinds her teeth.

Brain Booster #4

1. B
2. C
3. *Fly like an eagle* is a simile.
4. This passage is about the author's voyage on the *Kon-Tiki* with Thor Heyerdahl. They built the boat to be like prehistoric boats to prove people from South America could have gotten to Polynesia a long time ago.

Chapter 13: Cause and Effect

1. C
2. When scientists squeezed methane, it turned into black diamond dust.
3. Answers will vary. Here is one possible answer: They would probably be rich because diamonds are so valuable.
4. A
5. B
6. D
7. You can stop an ice cream headache by warming up the ice cream on your tongue before swallowing it.

Chapter 14: Graphic Organizers and Pictures

1. B
2. A
3. D
4. The Australian numbat and the giant pangolin both like to slurp up termites with their tongues.
5. Annika Irmler has a very long tongue—it's seven centimeters long!
6. The filled-in graphic organizer should have "*Steamboat Willie* was made" after 1928 and "*The Simpsons* came out" after 1989.

Chapter 15: Finding Out More

1. D
2. C
3. B
4. B
5. The main idea is that Earth is very interesting under the surface. Near the hydrothermal vents, which begin under the ocean, there are all kinds of weird creatures that make the ocean floor look like another planet.
6. If I wanted to find out about deep holes, I would go to the library and look up "holes" and "core samples" in the dictionary. I would also look in magazines and newspapers to find articles about new holes.

Brain Booster #5

1. "Around three pounds" should be written under "Human Brain Weight."
2. B
3. A
4. Whales sleep with one eye closed because they rest only one side of their brains at a time. They can't sleep completely because then they couldn't breathe.

Practice Test

Introduction to the *Know It All!* Practice Test

By now you've reviewed all the important skills that you should know for elementary school reading. You know the difference between fact and opinion (Chapter 4). You recognize the handful of important literary and poetic devices—things that writers use to make their writing interesting and fun (Chapters 9 and 10). You learned about the major elements of a story (Chapter 12). And these are just a few examples that don't even include all the excellent tidbits of information you've picked up. You *know it all!*

If you're ready, it's time to try out the skills from the fifteen chapters in this book on a practice test. This test may be similar to a test you take in class. It contains both multiple-choice and open-response questions.

Each multiple-choice question on the test has four answer choices. You should fill in the bubble for the correct answer choice on the separate answer sheet. Cut or tear out the answer sheet on the next page, and use it for the multiple-choice questions. You can write your answers to the open-response questions directly onto the test.

The practice test contains twenty-eight questions, eighteen of which are multiple choice. Give yourself ninety minutes to complete the test.

Take the practice test the same way you would take an actual test. Don't watch television, don't talk on the telephone, and don't listen to music while you take the test. Sit at a desk with a few pencils, and have an adult time you if possible. Take the test all in one sitting. If you break up the test in parts, you won't get a real test-taking experience.

When you've completed the practice test, you may go to page 173 to check your answers. Each question also has an explanation to help you understand how to answer it correctly. Don't look at that part of the book until you've finished the test!

Good luck!

Know It All! Answer Sheet

Name _____

1. Ⓐ Ⓑ Ⓒ Ⓓ

2. Ⓐ Ⓑ Ⓒ Ⓓ

3. Ⓐ Ⓑ Ⓒ Ⓓ

4. Use space provided.

5. Ⓐ Ⓑ Ⓒ Ⓓ

6. Ⓐ Ⓑ Ⓒ Ⓓ

7. Ⓐ Ⓑ Ⓒ Ⓓ

8. Use space provided.

9. Use space provided.

10. Ⓐ Ⓑ Ⓒ Ⓓ

11. Ⓐ Ⓑ Ⓒ Ⓓ

12. Ⓐ Ⓑ Ⓒ Ⓓ

13. Use space provided.

14. Ⓐ Ⓑ Ⓒ Ⓓ

15. Ⓐ Ⓑ Ⓒ Ⓓ

16. Ⓐ Ⓑ Ⓒ Ⓓ

17. Use space provided.

18. Use space provided.

19. Ⓐ Ⓑ Ⓒ Ⓓ

20. Ⓐ Ⓑ Ⓒ Ⓓ

21. Ⓐ Ⓑ Ⓒ Ⓓ

22. Use space provided.

23. Use space provided.

24. Ⓐ Ⓑ Ⓒ Ⓓ

25. Ⓐ Ⓑ Ⓒ Ⓓ

26. Ⓐ Ⓑ Ⓒ Ⓓ

27. Use space provided.

28. Use space provided.

Sample Questions

Directions: Read the passages and the questions that go with the passage. Mark the answers to multiple-choice questions on your bubble sheet. Write your answers to open-response questions in the space provided on the test.

The Gray House?

 The White House is the home of the president of the United States. But some say the White House wasn't always white and that when it was first built, it was gray.

The White House was built in 1792–1800 and was made mostly out of gray sandstone. The first president to move in was John Adams with his wife, Abigail. Thomas Jefferson was the first president to open the White House to tours, and it has been open to the public ever since.

During the War of 1812, the White House was burned by British troops. When the building was fixed after the fire, it was painted white to hide the smoke stains.

The White House had several different names in the early days, including the President's Palace and the Executive Mansion. President Theodore Roosevelt gave the home the name *White House* in 1901.

▶ Who was the first president to live in the White House?

A   George Washington
B   Thomas Jefferson
C   John Adams
D   Theodore Roosevelt

▶ According to the passage, why is the White House white?

_____

_____

_____

Brutus the Skydiving Dog

 Some dogs like to eat slippers. Some dogs like to chase cars. Some dogs even like to have jobs, such as helping blind people or searching for lost children. Brutus the skydiving dog, well, he likes to jump out of airplanes . . . with a parachute, of course!

Brutus is a little brown dachshund with floppy ears and a curious expression on his face. His owner's name is Ron Sirull. When Brutus makes his jumps, he is actually safely tucked into a pouch that is fastened to Ron's chest. The two go up in the airplane together, and when they are high enough, they jump. Then they open the parachute and drift to the ground, looking out over the wide world on the way down.

By the age of four, Brutus had jumped out of a plane one hundred times. And in 1997, Brutus reached a very important goal that he had been working toward his entire life. Brutus became the world's "Highest Skydiving Dog" at that time by jumping out of a plane that was fifteen thousand feet above the ground.

Now Brutus lives the life of the celebrity by appearing on TV shows and being written about in magazines. Will all of the fame change him? Well, that remains to be seen. Hopefully Brutus will always just be good old floppy-eared Brutus, the skydiving dog.

Directions: Answer questions 1–4 about the passage "Brutus the Skydiving Dog."

1. According to the passage, what does Brutus like to do best?

   A   chase cars
   B   help blind people
   C   jump out of airplanes
   D   look for missing children

2. Why do you think the writer wrote this story?

   A   to inform people about the dangers of skydiving
   B   to entertain people with a story about a funny dog
   C   to explain to people how to teach their pets to skydive
   D   to persuade people that dogs are happier if they have jobs

3. Which of the following best describes what Brutus's life is like after he became famous?

   A   Brutus is like a celebrity.
   B   Brutus became bored of parachuting.
   C   Brutus got a new owner.
   D   Brutus tries all kinds of other stunts.

4. What does Brutus look like? Write your answer in a complete sentence using details from the passage.

   _____

   _____

   _____

The First Floating Flights of Fancy

Humankind has always been fascinated by flight. Throughout history, people have tried to figure out how to fly like the birds they saw soaring so high in the air. Today, there are all kinds of ways to fly—airplanes, helicopters, and gliders can all give people the experience of flight.

Parachutes also let people (and dogs!) jump out of airplanes and float through the air. Even though people usually use airplanes to jump with parachutes today, it is interesting to note that parachutes were invented a very long time before airplanes even existed.

Leonardo da Vinci, a painter and sculptor who lived during the late 1400s, drew a sketch in his notebook of a man floating to the earth attached to a pyramid-shaped parachute. While da Vinci is said to be the first person to think of the idea of a parachute, he never actually tried it out.

Other inventors tried different types of parachutes over the years. In 1617, Faust Veranzio jumped off a tower in Venice, a city in Italy. He used a parachute a lot like the one in da Vinci's drawing. In 1783, Sebastian Lenormaud tried a jump off a tower with a fourteen-foot-wide parachute.

It wasn't until 1797 when Andrew Garnerin made several parachute jumps out of a hot air balloon that a parachute similar to the ones we have today was made. Garnerin used cloth instead of a stiff, wood frame for his parachutes. His jumps out of a hot air balloon were as high as eight thousand feet, which was a record height at that time.

When Garnerin jumped, however, he and his parachute would swing around wildly in the air. These uncontrollable swings were a problem. Eventually, with the advice of a French astronomer, Garnerin cut a hole, or a vent, at the top of his parachute. This stopped much of the swinging. Today's parachutes all have a vent in the top, even the ones used by Brutus the skydiving dog.

Other ideas, like using silk cloth to make parachutes and figuring out ways to steer them, have made parachutes easier to use. Parachuting is common as a hobby today, thanks to da Vinci and to the people who bravely tried them out a long time ago.

5. Which of these is found in the title of the passage?

    A   simile
    B   metaphor
    C   alliteration
    D   rhyme

6. Which statement best expresses the main idea of the passage?

    A   Leonardo da Vinci was an excellent artist who lived during the 1400s.
    B   Many people throughout history worked on developing the parachute.
    C   Parachutes are very colorful as they float down from the sky.
    D   Without airplanes, the parachute never would have been made.

7. What is the best meaning of the word *sketch,* as used in paragraph 3?

    A   graph
    B   letter
    C   painting
    D   drawing

8. According to the passage, what helps stop the parachute from swinging as it falls?

    _____

    _____

    _____

9. Use information from the story to complete the timeline below.

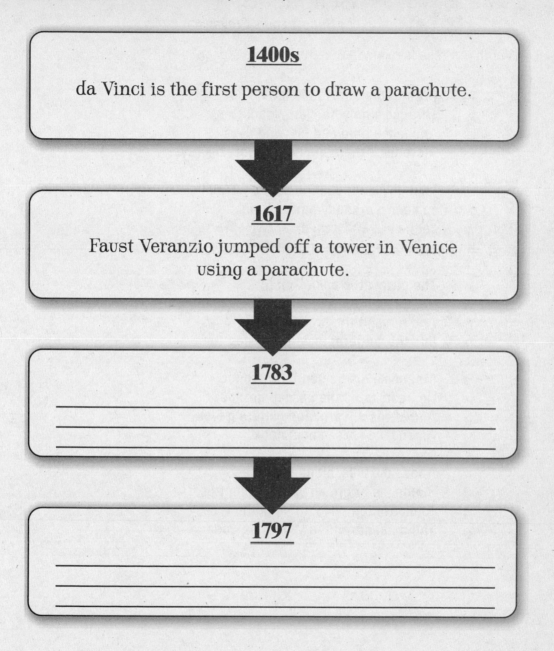

1400s

da Vinci is the first person to draw a parachute.

1617

Faust Veranzio jumped off a tower in Venice
using a parachute.

1783

_____

_____

_____

1797

_____

_____

_____

Summer Sun
by Robert Louis Stevenson

1   Great is the sun, and wide he goes

2   Through empty heaven without repose;

3   And in the blue and glowing days

4   More thick than rain he showers his rays.

5   Though closer still the blinds we pull

6   To keep our shady parlour cool,

7   Yet he will find a chink or two

8   To slip his golden fingers through.

9   The dusty attic spider-clad

10   He, through the keyhole, maketh glad;

11   And through the broken edge of tiles,

12   Into the laddered hay-loft smiles.

13   Meantime his golden face around

14   He bears to all the garden ground,

15   And sheds a warm and glittering look

16   Among the ivy's inmost nook.

17   Above the hills, along the blue,

18   Round the bright air with footing true,

19   To please the child, to paint the rose,

20   The gardener of the World, he goes.

Directions: Answer questions 10–13 about the poem "Summer Sun."

10. How many stanzas are in the poem?

    A 3

    B 4

    C 5

    D 6

11. Which of the following words in the poem rhyme?

    A *tiles* and *smiles*

    B *goes* and *days*

    C *ground* and *look*

    D *blue* and *rose*

12. Which of these lines from the poem shows an example of personification?

    A *And in the blue and glowing days*

    B *Though closer still the blinds we pull*

    C *To slip his golden fingers through*

    D *To keep our shady parlour cool*

13. What is the main idea of this poem?

    _____

    _____

    _____

Human Penguins

 If you've ever gone swimming in the ocean, you know that it can sometimes be pretty cold, even in the summer. The temperature of the Atlantic Ocean off the coast of Massachusetts can reach sixty or seventy degrees Fahrenheit in the summer. But in the winter, the temperature of the ocean is barely around forty degrees. Brrrrrr! Who wants to swim in that?

Well, Lynne Cox does, for one. She swam in the freezing cold water as comfortably as a polar bear.

Cox, a swimmer from New Hampshire, has swum in the coldest waters in the world. She swam across the Strait of Magellan off the coast of southern Chile. She swam the five miles from Alaska to Siberia in forty-degree water. The coldest swim by far was when Cox swam a little over a mile in the waters of Antarctica, which were thirty-two degrees! Some swimmers wear a wet suit or smear themselves with grease when they swim in cold water, but not Cox. She had on only a bathing suit, a cap, and goggles.

Another famous swimmer, Gertrude Ederle, was the first woman to ever swim across the English Channel in the year 1926. She completed the twenty-one-mile swim across the Channel in a little more than fourteen hours. It's pretty impressive to be able to swim that long in the ocean.

Ederle protected herself from the cold by covering her entire body with a layer of lard, olive oil, Vaseline, and lanolin. When she emerged from the water after her swim, she looked very goopy.

Both of these female swimmers have inspired people with their successes. Lynne Cox was named Woman of the Year by the *Los Angeles Times* and has been written about in a number of other magazines. After Gertrude Ederle swam across the English Channel, more women than ever before took up the sport of swimming.

Directions: Answer questions 14–18 about the passage "Human Penguins."

14. What does the following sentence from the passage show an example of?

   She swam in the freezing cold water as comfortably as a polar bear.

   A   simile
   B   metaphor
   C   alliteration
   D   personification

15. Which of the following statements from the passage is an opinion?
   A   *She swam the five miles from Alaska to Siberia in forty-degree water.*
   B   *She completed the twenty-one-mile swim across the Channel in a little more than fourteen hours.*
   C   *It's pretty impressive to be able to swim that long in the ocean.*
   D   *Cox, a swimmer from New Hampshire, has swum in the coldest waters in the world.*

16. In this sentence from the passage, what does the word *emerged* mean?

   When she emerged from the water after her swim, she looked very goopy.

   A   fell asleep
   B   smiled
   C   put on grease
   D   came out

17. What are two places where Lynne Cox swam?

   _____

   _____

18. Complete this Venn diagram comparing and contrasting Lynne Cox and Gertrude Ederle.

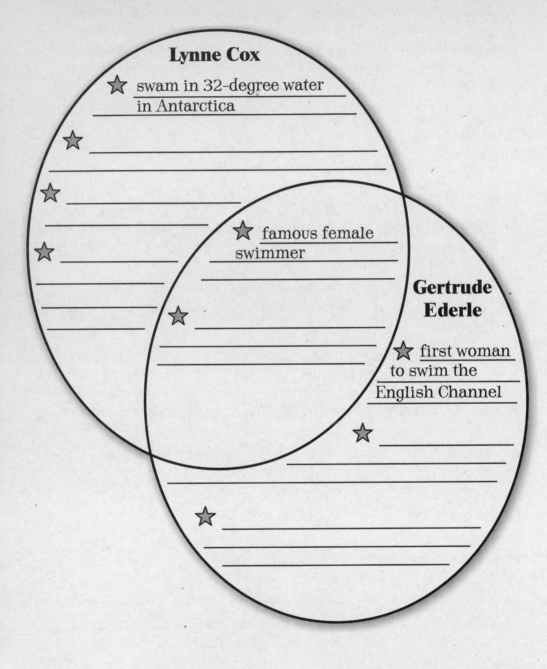

Lynne Cox

⭐ swam in 32-degree water in Antarctica

⭐ _____

⭐ _____

⭐ _____

⭐ famous female swimmer

⭐ _____

Gertrude Ederle

⭐ first woman to swim the English Channel

⭐ _____

⭐ _____

The Tunnels of Turpan

Little Kamile lived with her family in a town called Turpan. Turpan is in the middle of Central Asia, near the Tian Shan Mountains and surrounded by the desert. Kamile lived on a great grape farm, and her family grew the juiciest, fattest grapes in the entire region.

Everyone in Kamile's family liked to take walks in the desert after dinner. The air was much cooler than it was during the day, and softer, too. During the day, the desert air was very hot and dry, and the sun was an eye staring down always paying attention to what you were doing. "Are you working?" the sun would say. "Are you working? Work! Work!" During the day everyone in Kamile's family worked very hard, and so did Kamile. But at night, they could rest and walk about in the soothing privacy of the night.

After the evening stroll, Kamile's family dropped into bed and slept like still desert rocks. Kamile, on the other hand, couldn't sleep at all. She was kept awake by the sound of water rushing past their house in one of the swiftly moving canals the family used to water their fields of grapes.

One day, Kamile complained about the rushing water to her mother. "Ma," she said, "I don't like living here. Not. At. All." Kamile was whining just a little bit, but she was very tired from not sleeping.

"Why not?" her mother asked, a little bit annoyed because Kamile had everything you could ever need—a nice family, food, and even some toys.

"Well," said Kamile, "I can't ever sleep at night because the water rushing through the canals is so loud that it keeps me awake."

"I don't think you know how important those water canals are." Kamile's Ma was a little angry at Kamile. "Those water canals keep us alive."

Kamile's Ma explained why the water canals were so important. Because Turpan was in the middle of such a huge desert, nothing would be able to grow because there was no water. Thousands of years ago, the people who lived there worked very hard to build underground tunnels that bring water from the faraway snow-covered mountains. These tunnels kept the water from sinking into the ground so it could travel hundreds of miles through the desert to Turpan.

"Oh," Kamile understood. "So if that water wasn't rushing by and keeping me awake, we wouldn't have our grape fields. In fact, we wouldn't have anything!"

"That's right," said her Ma.

After that day, Kamile never had another sleepless night because she would listen to the water rushing by and feel so happy that it was there to help her family.

Directions: Answer questions 19–23 about the passage "The Tunnels of Turpan."

19. What is the point of view of this passage?

    A It is a story told in the first person.

    B It is an autobiography about the author's life.

    C The narrator is telling the story in the third person.

    D It is a letter written in the second person.

20. Which of these statements best tells the theme of the story?

    A Appreciate what you have.

    B Haste makes waste.

    C Shortcuts cause long delays.

    D Beauty is only skin deep.

21. What is one way that Kamile is different from the rest of her family?

    A Kamile likes to swim in the canals.

    B Kamile works much harder than her family.

    C Kamile doesn't like to walk in the desert.

    D Kamile can't sleep very well at night.

22. Write one metaphor from the story.

_____

_____

_____

23. What is the plot of this story? Write a short summary using complete sentences.

_____

_____

_____

_____

_____

Delicious Moldy Snacks

 Have you ever noticed that when bread has been on the counter for too long it starts to grow mold? Moldy bread is pretty gross—it has a greenish-gray fuzz growing all over it. Yuck! Food often gets moldy if it has been left uneaten for too long, especially if it is in a wet place. This is because mold spores that float around in the air can fall on damp food and start to grow. Mold can't get energy from the sun, so it has to get energy by eating other foods. While it might be nasty to find mold on your food, in nature, mold is useful because it helps to rot food, which in turn returns nutrients to the soil for other things to grow out of.

There are some foods in your refrigerator that are supposed to be moldy and they taste yummy that way, like cheese. Blue cheese has mold growing in it—that's what makes the blue lines in the cheese and gives it a delicious, sharp flavor. Many cheeses are stored, or ripened, for a long time to allow molds to grow in and around the soft center. If you see a kind of cheese with a gray crust surrounding a soft white center, the gray part is mostly made of mold. Yum! These kinds of cheeses are delicious.

When Swiss cheese is made, it is bacteria, as well as mold, that is an important part of the cheese-making process. When Swiss cheese is ripened, an added type of bacteria eats the lactic acid that is produced in the ripening process. Then the bacteria give off lots of carbon dioxide gas, which collects in pockets and makes the big holes that you see in Swiss cheese.

So the next time you see a gross, squishy, moldy lemon in your refrigerator, remember how important mold is for many reasons, including for making yummy cheese. Plus, the next time you have a grilled cheese sandwich for lunch, and someone asks you what you are having, you can say, "Mold!"

Directions: Answer questions 24–28 about the passage "Delicious Moldy Snacks."

24. What happens to some food that has been left uneaten for too long?

    A It releases spores into the air.
    B It develops holes on the inside.
    C It gets eaten by your hungry friend.
    D It grows a greenish-gray fuzz on it.

25. What is **not** mentioned in the article as a benefit of mold?

    A Cheese is made up partially of mold.
    B Mold helps return nutrients to the soil.
    C Mold makes old food in the fridge taste better.
    D The yummy crust of some cheese is made of mold.

26. If you don't like sharp cheese, and you want to find a word that means the opposite of *sharp,* what resource can help you?

    A thesaurus
    B atlas
    C almanac
    D dictionary

27. What causes mold to grow on some foods?

   _____

   _____

   _____

28. What do the added bacteria in Swiss cheese do in the cheese-making process?

   _____

   _____

   _____

Answers and Explanations for the Practice Test

1. **C** This question asks about a detail from the passage. The first paragraph talks about what some dogs like to do, including what Brutus likes to do. Find the answer choice that matches what Brutus likes to do. Does he like to chase cars, as in answer choice (A)? Well, some dogs like to chase cars, but the passage does not say that Brutus likes to chase cars in particular. Cross off (A). Some dogs also like to have jobs like helping blind people and looking for missing children, as in answer choices (B) and (D), but Brutus is not mentioned as doing any of those jobs. The entire passage is about how Brutus likes to skydive, or jump out of airplanes, so answer choice (C) is correct.

2. **B** Think about the answer to this question in your own words. What do you think the purpose of the passage is? Well, the passage was fun to read and told you some fun stuff about a dog. So the purpose was probably to entertain the reader. Check the answer choices to find which one matches.

   Answer choice (A) has to do with informing the reader about the dangers of skydiving, not entertaining the reader. Cross off (A). Answer choice (B) is about entertaining the reader, so it is most likely the correct answer. Hold on to (B) but check the others to be sure. Answer choice (C) has to do with explaining how to teach pets to skydive, so that one isn't correct either. Answer choice (D) is about showing the reader that pets really are happy when they have jobs. That's not the answer you had in mind either. Answer choice (B) is correct.

3. **A** The last paragraph contains details about Brutus's life after he became famous. He appears on TV shows and in magazines just like a celebrity. He is famous! The passage does not say that Brutus ever got bored of parachutes (can dogs even get bored?). He also didn't get a new owner or try new stunts.

4. This is an open-response question that asks you to describe Brutus. Use details from the passage and be sure to write in complete sentences and check your work. Here is an example of a good response.

   Brutus is small and brown with floppy ears and a curious expression on his face.

5. **C** Say the title of the passage to yourself and listen to the sounds. Remember that alliteration is when the sounds at the beginnings of words all sound the same. That's what you will hear in the title. Similes, answer choice (A), and metaphors, answer choice (B), are types of comparisons that do not appear in the title. Rhyme, answer choice (D), is when the sounds at the ends of the words are alike. In the title, it is the sounds at the beginning of the words, not at the ends, that are alike.

6. **B** This is a main idea question. Think about what the passage is mostly about. The passage is mostly about the history of the parachute and all the people who built them or tried them out. Look through the answer choices to find the one that matches this idea. Be careful not to choose a response that is only a detail from the passage. Answer choice (A) is a detail about Leonardo da Vinci, so you can cross it out. Answer choice (B) mentions the history of the parachute. (B) seems correct, but check the rest of the answer choices just to be sure. Answer choice (C) mentions a detail—the colors of parachutes—but that isn't even in the passage, so you can definitely cross that one off. Answer choice (D) is a detail that is not correct because the passage states that the parachute was invented before the airplane. This means that airplanes were not necessary for the invention of the parachute. Answer choice (B) is correct.

7. **D** This is a vocabulary-in-context question. Find the sentence in paragraph 3 in which the word *sketch* appears. (You can also look at the drawing that goes with the passage for help.) Replace the word *sketch* in the sentence with each answer choice to see which one fits. Did da Vinci draw a *graph* in his notebook of a man? No, this doesn't fit. Cross off (A). Did he draw a *letter*? Well, letters are usually written, not drawn, so you can cross off (B). Did he draw a *painting*? If he did, the sentence would probably use the verb *painted,* not *draw.* You can cross off (C). Da Vinci drew a *drawing* in his notebook—answer choice (D) is correct.

8. This open-response question asks you about a detail from the passage. You can find the information in the second to last paragraph of the passage. Here is an example of a good response.

A parachute has a hole, or vent, in the top to keep it from swinging.

9.

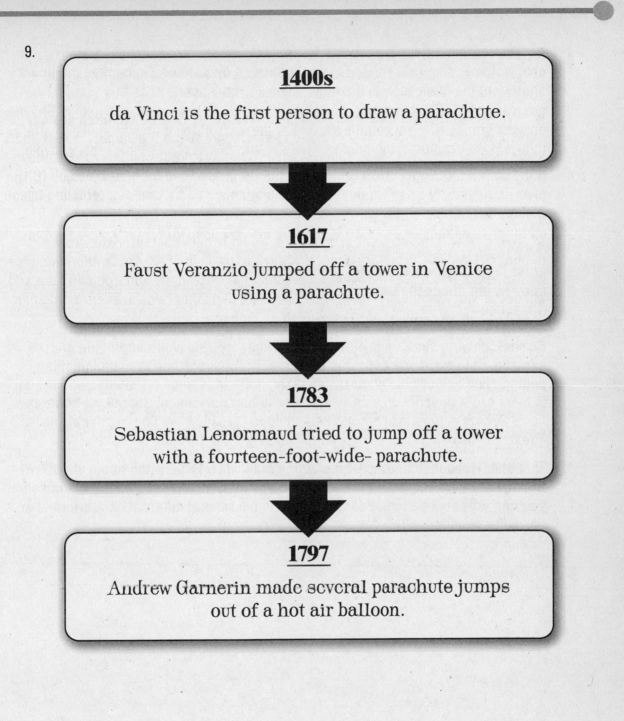

1400s

da Vinci is the first person to draw a parachute.

1617

Faust Veranzio jumped off a tower in Venice using a parachute.

1783

Sebastian Lenormaud tried to jump off a tower with a fourteen-foot-wide- parachute.

1797

Andrew Garnerin made several parachute jumps out of a hot air balloon.

10. **C** You need to remember what a stanza is to answer this question. A stanza is a group of lines in a poem. Stanzas are separated by a space. Go back to the poem and count the stanzas. There are five stanzas in the poem.

11. **A** When words rhyme, their endings sound the same. Go through each answer choice and say the words in your head to see if they sound the same. Do *tiles* and *smiles* sound the same? Yes. Hold on to (A). What about *goes* and *days*? No, they don't sound the same. Cross off (B). Neither do *ground* and *look,* so cross off (C) also. *Blue* and *rose* don't sound alike, although it would be kind of interesting to see a blue rose! Cross off (D) as well.

12. **C** Remember that personification means giving human characteristics to nonhuman things. This entire poem is really an example of personification because it talks about the sun as if it were a person. It talks about the sun's golden face and about the sun walking the Earth and doing nice things for people. Every single line doesn't have an example of personification, though.

"…and glowing days…" is an example of imagery—days are often blue and glowing, but people are not. "The blinds we pull" is referring to actual people pulling blinds closed, so no personification there. Keeping "the shady parlour cool" is a concrete description, not an example of personification. But talking about the sun's fingers is personification! The sun doesn't really have fingers, people do. These words describe the rays of light coming from the sun.

13. This open-response question asks for the main idea. What is the poem about? Because poems can have different meanings for different people, this is a question you can probably get credit for by answering in several different ways. Here is a possible response:

The poem is about how the summer sun makes people feel good.

14. **A**   Do you remember all of the terms for literary devices? This sentence contains an example of a simile. You can tell this because the sentence compares Lynne Cox to a polar bear and uses the word *as.* A metaphor is a comparison that would not contain *as.* Alliteration doesn't compare two things. Personification can give human qualities to animals, but this sentence gives animal qualities to a human, which is not personification. And there is no such thing as animalification!

15. **C**   This is a fact-versus-opinion question. You need to find the statement that is an opinion. Go through the answer choices and cross off the ones that are facts. Answer choice (A) is a fact because it states how far Lynne Cox swam and how cold the water was. These are facts that can be checked. Answer choice (B) is a fact because it talks about how far Gertrude Ederle swam and how long it took her. You can also check that. Answer choice (C) is an opinion because some people might not agree that it is impressive to swim that long in the ocean. Answer choice (D) can also be checked—it is a fact that Lynne Cox is a swimmer from New Hampshire and that she has swum in the coldest waters in the world.

16. **D**   This is a vocabulary-in-context question. Go through each answer choice to see if the definition makes sense in the sentence. Would Ederle look goopy if she fell asleep in the water? Well, she never would even have made it across the English Channel if she had fallen asleep. Cross off (A). Did she smile? She probably did smile when she was finally finished with her swim, but this does not explain why she would be so goopy. Cross off (B). Ederle also put on grease before her swim, not after her swim, so answer choice (C) doesn't make sense. Answer choice (D) is correct—when she *came out* of the water after her swim, she looked pretty goopy!

17. This is an open-response question that asks you to write two places where Lynne Cox swam. The passage mentions more than two—the Strait of Magellan in Chile, from Alaska to Siberia, and Antarctica—but you need to only write two. Write your answer in a complete sentence. Here is an example.

Lynne Cox swam across the Strait of Magellan in Chile, and she swam in Antarctica.

18.

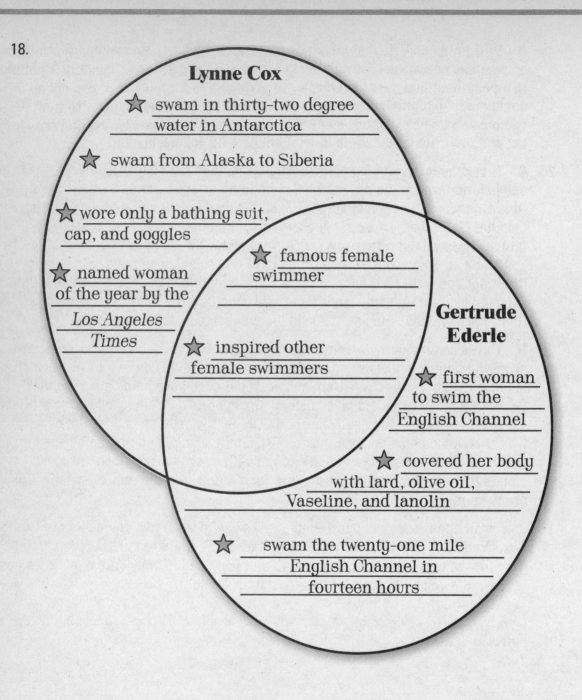

Lynne Cox

⭐ swam in thirty-two degree water in Antarctica

⭐ swam from Alaska to Siberia

⭐ wore only a bathing suit, cap, and goggles

⭐ named woman of the year by the *Los Angeles Times*

⭐ famous female swimmer

⭐ inspired other female swimmers

Gertrude Ederle

⭐ first woman to swim the English Channel

⭐ covered her body with lard, olive oil, Vaseline, and lanolin

⭐ swam the twenty-one mile English Channel in fourteen hours

19. **C** This question asks about the point of view of the story. Remember that the point of view has to do with how the narrator is looking at the story. This story is not told by any of the characters in the story, so you can cross off (A). It is also not an autobiography of the author's life, because Kamile is not the author. Cross off (B). The passage is not a letter, so (D) is also incorrect. The narrator is telling the story about Kamile from the outside. Answer choice (C) is correct.

20. **A** The theme of a story gives a broad statement of what a passage is about. The theme of the passage can be what the characters learn in the passage. The theme can also sound like a proverb. What does Kamile learn in this story? She learns that the water that annoys her is very important to the lives of her family. She learns to appreciate what the water does, because it keeps her family alive.

    The expression "Haste makes waste" means that if you do something too fast, it might ruin it. The expression "Shortcuts make long delays" means that if you try to cheat and do something quicker, it might actually take you a lot longer. The expression "Beauty is only skin deep" means that a beautiful person isn't always a good person.

21. **D** Kamile and her family are similar in many ways. In the second paragraph of the story, the narrator says that Kamile and her family all like to walk in the desert and they all work very hard. You can cross off (B) and (C). Answer choice (A), Kamile likes to swim in the canals, can also be crossed off because this detail is not mentioned in the passage.

22. This open-response question asks for a metaphor from the story. A metaphor is a comparison between two things. A metaphor does not use *like* or *as*—similes use these words. There is only one metaphor in this story, comparing the sun to a glowing eye. Here is how you can write your answer.

There is a metaphor in the passage that compares the sun to a glowing eye.

23. This open-response question asks for the summary of the plot. The plot tells what happens in a story, and because it is a summary, you need to tell only the main points. In a question like this, it is often possible to get partial credit, so answer as much as you can. Here is one possible answer.

This is a story about Kamile, who lives in the desert with her family. Kamile doesn't like the sound of the water rushing by her house because it keeps her awake at night. She complains to her mother about the noise, but her mother gets mad. Her mother tells Kamile that the water rushing by is very important to their lives. The water makes it possible for them to live in the desert. After that, Kamile can sleep because she knows the water is helping them.

24. **D** This question asks you for a detail from the passage. Think of the answer to the question in your own words and then read through the answer choices carefully. The passage says that food that has been left out starts to grow mold. Does the passage mention that food that has been left uneaten releases spores into the air? No. Cross off (A). Does uneaten food grow holes? The passage talks about holes forming in Swiss cheese but not in uneaten food. Cross off (B) too. Does the old food get eaten by your hungry friend? Hopefully not! Well, the passage doesn't mention that either, so (C) can be crossed off. Answer choice (D) says that the food grows a greenish-gray fuzz, which is how the passage describes mold. So this one matches your answer.

25. **C** The word *not* is very important in this question. You need to find something that is not mentioned in the passage. The passage talks about how cheese has mold, and sometimes the crust is mold. It also says that mold helps return nutrients to the soil. The passage suggests that moldy food is gross, actually, and does not make food taste better at all. So this is the opposite of what is mentioned in the passage.

26. **A** This question asks you about finding information in a resource book. It helps to remember the terms from Chapter 15. A thesaurus is the best resource for finding the opposites of words. An atlas has maps, an almanac has information about the weather, and a dictionary gives you the definitions of words.

27. This is a cause-and-effect question. You need to go back to the passage to find the information about what causes mold to grow on some foods. This information can be found in the first paragraph. Mold grows on some food when mold spores land on food that has been left out for too long. A damp environment is a good place for mold to grow. Here is an example of how you might respond to this question.

Mold grows on some foods when it has been left out too long. Mold spores that float around in the air land on the left-out food. If the food is in a wet place, mold is more likely to grow on the food.

28. This open-response question asks you for a detail from the passage. In the third paragraph, you can find information about what bacteria do to Swiss cheese— bacteria eat lactic acid, and then give off gas that makes the holes in the cheese. Here's one way to answer this question.

The bacteria added to Swiss cheese eat lactic acid and give off gas. The gas collects in pockets to make the holes that Swiss cheese is known for.

The Princeton Review

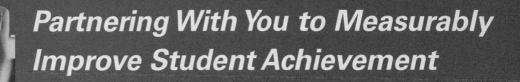

Partnering With You to Measurably Improve Student Achievement

Our proven 3-step approach lets you **assess** student performance, **analyze** the results, and **act** to improve every student's mastery of skills covered by your State Standards.

Assess
Deliver formative and benchmark tests

Analyze
Review in-depth performance reports and implement ongoing professional development

Act
Utilize after school programs, course materials, and enrichment resources

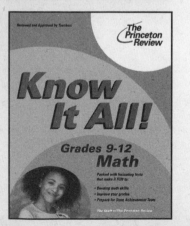